THE COMPLETE TIPS
FOR ACTORS

THE COMPLETE TIPS
FOR ACTORS

Smith and Kraus Publishers

2013

ISBN 9781575258539
Library of Congress Control Number: 2013942859

Typesetting and layout by Elizabeth E. Monteleone
Cover by Borderlands Press

A Smith and Kraus book
177 Lyme Road, Hanover, NH 03755
editorial 603.643.6431 To Order 1.877.668.8680
www.smithandkraus.com

Printed in the United States of America

For Marcia Jory above all
And Zan Sawyer-Daily

THE DIRECTOR

No-No's

PEOPLE STUFF

Tips. The way 90 percent of all acting knowledge gets communicated. My mother and father (actors for over fifty years) would finish the play, repair to a bar with the cast, and my father, surveying the table, would ask, "Any tips for me tonight?" The table was then open for business. There would be talk about laughs that had been lost, builds that didn't function, entrances that should be delayed a half-beat, moments that should be underplayed and subtext that wasn't clear (though they didn't call it that, of course). School was open for the actors. The University of the Tip!

It still works that way. Often, it's a word to the wise in the green room or over a beer in the bar. Sometimes it's a whispered conversation with a veteran actor just outside the rehearsal room. Somebody has a little practical advice about a moment or a scene, or they remind you of some basic truth you've forgotten in the heat of battle. They pass on something they heard from an ancient character man who heard it from John Barrymore's dresser who heard it from someone who had heard it from Edwin Booth. The long, long chain of tips.

When you get into the all-consuming white-hot heat of working on a role, and the old can't-see-the-forest-for-the-trees loss of objectivity sets in, you may not have the time or inclination to re-read all of Stanislavski, and Peter Brook is stimulating but maybe a little vague on the details, and the director...well, the two of you maybe lack a little something in chemistry and communication., it might be that what you need is a "tip." The good tip either clears up the problem immediately, stimulates you to find a solution, or points out some work you need to do to break out of your double bind.

In this book, you will find a slew of them. They range all the way from defining that pesky word "action," to discussing how to kill an unwanted laugh, getting the focus when you need it, talking to the fight choreographer about a dangerous moment, dealing with a "diva," or finding the subtext under the innocuous line. Somewhere in here is the solution to what's nagging you in rehearsal or performance. And the good news right now is they are short, clear, and useful. As far as stimulation goes, the tips are hopefully like the sand in the oyster...just enough to get you going on a new tack (pearl to arrive shortly).

Dip in and open some new doors.

—Jon Jory

Ah, yes, the "user's guide." You could read it cover to cover, but it's pretty tightly packed, and that might be a little like drinking several espressos at a sitting. Take it to rehearsal and, in your downtime, skim until you're engaged by an idea. Take it home and skim until something relates to the day's rehearsal. Take it to your dressing room and, while you wait for your second act entrance, skim until it opens a closed moment for you. Take it class and see if it doesn't motivate you to try something new.

The book is broken down into general categories of related tips, everything from breaking down text, to using space, to building the role. An interest in one may carry you through the entire section, but the basic idea here is tip dipping.

If you've had a pretty good training or you've been working as an actor or director for awhile, you've run across a high percentage of this stuff elsewhere. But can you access it? Is it there when you need it? Do you not occasionally fail to act on it under the pressures of rehearsal or performance?

These are tools and stimuli, and much as the good carpenter needs a belt for them so they will be easy at hand, you should keep this book nearby. Like your notebook, your script, your highlighter, pencil and pen, your gaffer's tape and your blocking notation, it's meant to be practical—it's meant to do a job for you.

This is the voice of the old theatre rat whispering in your ear on a five-minute break. This is the impasse breaker, the horizon scanner, the kick-starter and the how-the-hell-did-I-forget-that tickler. Like all creative tools, it's not a how-to, it's a how-maybe-to. It's the common wisdom.

A quick note on using tips in the classroom. I have heard from a number of teachers that they begin and finish classes with a reading of a "tip" and a short discussion. The tip is chosen for its connections to the acting problems being addressed. For more specific classroom exercises I would refer you to my book "Teaching the Actor Craft." It covers fifty areas of acting study with several dialogue exercises and coaching tips for each.

AN ACTION

Whole tomes are written on the action. Whole theories make it central. Every actor claims to use them. Why then do they seem so often absent? To remind us, the action is either what you want the other person onstage to do, to feel, or to understand. If you're alone onstage, the action has the same definition only applied to you. Because large roles are made up of hundreds of actions, very few performers will do all that homework. Admit you are lazy and use them for spot work. This moment isn't working—what's the action? This beat seems unclear—what's the action? I feel self-conscious here—what's the action? For an action to be dramatic, it needs a counter-balancing obstacle; so make sure you know what it is. When you know the action and the obstacle and it still isn't working, raise the stakes. Simple as that.

ACTION II

This action: what you want the other to do, feel or understand, hopefully puts the scene between you. The action probably relates to the meaning of the scene or the theme of the play. If the action of the beat is, "I want him to kiss me," that's good because you will know when the action is completed. If, however, the action oversimplifies the intent of the moment, it will demean the scene. To further pursue the idea of the action, use the words "to what end?" The answer to the question, "I want him to kiss me, but to what end?" (no bawdry, please) will add a resonance to the acting. In a sense, every action contains philosophy and poetry; it is not simply the pursuit of a "square meal." By understanding not only the action's simplicity but its resonance, the acting will have weight and dimension. No action is graven in stone. You can try it and then change it. The action isn't a "result," it's an attempt. But have one.

The Obstacle

Here's one of the absolutely necessary key building blocks of performance. We know the action is what we want the other actor to do, but what obstacle prevents us from accomplishing that? In the theatre, every action has an obstacle or else the action is undramatic. To increase intensity, we look to make the obstacle even more daunting. Usually, unless you can articulate the obstacle, you won't be able to plan tactics to achieve your end. Sometimes the obstacle lies in the actor himself, sometimes outside him in another, or in a group or in a natural order or in society itself. Your problem in the scene may be none other than not having a sufficiently interesting obstacle. Another actor may not realize that they need to provide the obstacle, and if it isn't a relationship where you can discuss that, then you may have to reconceive the obstacle as lying in you or outside both of you. If you don't understand the obstacle, you may be pursuing the action in a way that is outside the circumstances or would simply make matters worse.

Action and Obstacle in Balance

The action: what you want the other character to do. The obstacle: what prevents that from happening. If the action is significantly stronger than the obstacle, it is achieved too easily and the result is undramatic. If the obstacle is too powerful, the action is too soon abandoned and the result is undramatic. Find a crucial beat. Define the action. Define the obstacle. Remember we don't pay to see a woman lift a Kleenex—we pay to see her lift a piano. We want these two crucial acting elements to achieve a fascinating balance, to almost (but not quite) force an impasse. When something isn't working, check this balance and increase one or the other until the moment teeters on the edge with something important to be won or lost. I relate to the moment where the Olympic lifter hoists the unbearable weight to waist level and, trembling with effort, prepares to move it above his head. He does. Now he will either collapse or achieve; either might happen. We are riveted and fascinated. The action and obstacle are in balance.

Beats

The beat is to acting as the paragraph is to writing. The beat changes when the subject (textual or sub-textual) changes. The beat is ordinarily defined not from your character's viewpoint but from the text's. Beats are ordinarily marked by the actor with brackets [ ]. The uses of marking the beats are many. It forces us to ask what is really going on before we can identify it. It helps us understand the text's rhythm and style as it would in music. It points out that a transition exists and must be played between beats. It gives us units of text that we can further analyze for context and structure. It makes clear when the action changes. Sometimes a beat may seem to be about going shopping but is really about the characters' relationship on a subtextual level. The beat then ends when the subtext changes. Beats strung end to end with different actions, obstacles, and tactics identified create the role's landscape. I know, I know, most books define beats as changing when the action changes. A perfectly good way to look at it.

Circumstances

These are not subjective opinions. These are facts in the text. It is six o'clock. It takes place in Las Vegas. Jack is a butcher, etc. Sit down and list them. Then ask questions of yourself to break them open. It says Bethany had an abortion. Ask why. Ask if religion affects her choice. Ask if anyone influenced her choice. Ask whatever strikes you as pertinent, answer and ask again until it creates a lake of information you can draw on in rehearsal. To break open a single circumstance may take a half-hour, so pick the most pertinent to work on if your time is limited. This is crucial work. If you don't understand the circumstances, you can't build the role appropriately or understand the rules of the text. Acting serves the text, and the text gives boundaries to the actor. Let's call these boundaries the rules. The circumstances are the rules for that particular play. We need the rules to do the work.

Jon Jory

TACTICS

The action is what your character wants another character to do. The tactic is how you get the other to do it. The action, as in Lopahin trying to get Madam Ranevskaya to sell the cherry orchard, may last for an entire play, but the tactics keep changing. The same thing is true in a single beat. Even in six lines there may be several changes of tactics. You may cajole, play on her sympathy, demand, and sulk all on a single page in the service of a single need. The more difficult the obstacle, the greater the number of tactics. The values to the actor of varying the tactics are many. On the simplest level, it provides crucial variety which is the staff of life for both the actor and the audience. Needing to change tactics is the sign of a good, juicy, frustrating obstacle that engages our full attention. Each change of tactic also provokes a new and different response from our scene partner which moves the scene forward. One warning: make sure the tactics are appropriate to the character and to your commonsense view of what people actually do in real circumstances.

SUBTEXT

Subtext is, obviously, what you really mean under what you say. You say, "I'm going to bed"; you mean, "I don't want to talk to you." Over the course of a career as a director, I've found that asking what the subtext is improves work more immediately than almost any other tool. Usually when you identify the subtext, you find it also describes an action and thus is doubly useful. While most actors use subtext consciously or unconsciously, they may not think to decode the other characters' unspoken intentions, which can unlock a recalcitrant scene. We not only speak code, we are always busy decoding one another's conversation, which deeply influences the way we relate to each other. If the scene is eluding you, write the subtext for the other character as well as your own, and see if it isn't wonderfully clarifying.

25

This is the difference between what your character wants and feels at the beginning and at the end. There's arc for the whole play, the act, the scene, and even the beat. Pick a section you are working on and think about it. Once you can articulate a starting and finishing point, look for the fulcrum moment where your character starts the journey away from "A" and begins the transformation to "B." Yes, you can go on a journey from Peoria to Peoria, but who wants to? And more importantly, who wants to see it? What really animates a major character is change. The arc helps define what that change is. When working on the play as a whole, it is valuable to start with the end, define it and then go back to the beginning and make sure it is situated differently. Remember that the arc can also be used on micro-sections for spot work. Arcs also enforce variety and give you the crucial sense of the role as a whole. Without it, you can get lost in the details.

Theme Threads

If you don't know what the play is about, how are you going to recognize the important moments? If you don't recognize the important moments, how are you going to act the part? Don't neglect the big picture. Theme threads are strings of meaning that run through the play. This is about loneliness, that's about loneliness, over here they mention loneliness. *Hmmm, could be a theme thread.* When you've identified five or six theme threads in the text and subtext, write them in order and see if you can think of a category that includes all or most of them. This is a central theme. Now take the theme to the text and identify moments that explicate the theme or theme threads. These are likely to be important moments—important to give focus to and play interestingly and well. The basic idea is that without a map of the big picture, it's difficult to make the little things work. You owe several hours to this process.

Jon Jory

TRANSITIONS

They exist at that moment where you move from one idea to another in your text. Usually they fall after a period (though every period doesn't mark a transition). The transition to a new idea may be signed by a pause (the mind changing direction), a physical move, or even a change in expression. They can be marked by a change of tone or rhythm. The important point is that the actor's physical and mental process mark them. I usually go through the text and indicate them with a slash mark. Won't your intuition take care of this? Probably not. I watch some very sophisticated actors running them like stop lights. Frankly, it's what I watch for most in auditions. Is this actor making the transitions? They are the chief sign of an inner life and text work at home. Great actors probably do them naturally. For the rest of us, we're probably going to need to add our conscious mind to the process. Transitions—the bridge to the next idea.

BACKSTORY

This is the character's offstage history, both mentioned in the text and imagined by the actor. Backstory helps you explain behavior, stimulates you emotionally and allows you to deepen and make more dramatic key moments and scenes. Don't develop the backstory until your character understanding is quite advanced. Use backstory to assist in clarifying your behavior. If you can't point to the line in the play that your backstory affects in a way that helps you make a point the playwright wants to make, don't go to the trouble. The wrong backstory produces the wrong moment. The childhood you imagine must produce the character the playwright imagines. Backstory is not playwriting, it is supportive evidence for the case the text makes. Don't play the character to support your backstory. Create the backstory to heighten circumstances clearly in the play—best done after a week of studying text and revised in rehearsal.

27

Mysteries

Not so long after you begin your textwork, or early in rehearsal, you're going to run into moments that seem opaque, impervious to your sense of the scene's logic, out of character for your character, and an improbable speech or activity given your grasp of the circumstances. Love and gather those moments. These are the places that will eventually break the play open for you. Worry these moments like a dog. Make lists of questions to ask about them and write down your answers. It is these mysteries, once known by you, that will make your acting in the role dimensional. Your character says, "I feel so alive," and shortly after commits suicide. Now here's a mystery. Alive in what sense? Alive because of what experience? The fact is that you can't act the play until you solve that moment. How does that moment relate to the end? What does this mystery have to do with the play's theme? Enjoy your frustration in confronting the mysteries. They are pure gold.

Personalization

No matter how astoundingly well written, all characters lack the complexity, the detailed history, the ambivalence and the sheer volume of details that your own life has. It is your life that makes your work in the role distinct and individual. We are there to see *Medea*, plus you. Bring your life to the table! By examining the character and the events of the play, and both comparing them to and understanding them through your own life, you personalize the role. By personalizing the role, you deepen your interest and desire to perform this particular part. You know full well that the greater your interest in a task, the better you do it. Once you have fully examined the circumstances in the text, find similar situations in your past. If not precisely similar in event, you can abstract the nature of the circumstance. You may not have killed, but you have been driven to do harm. This simple understanding of the moment in your own terms bonds you consciously and subconsciously with the part. Parallel experiences will sometimes provide you with what you might "do," and doing that often reclaims and releases in you the original emotion. The performance of the role is your own life examined in the light of the circumstances and central themes of the play. Add a dash of human characteristics that seem indicated by the text, and you are on your way.

WORKING BACKWARDS

After you've read the play three or four times (twice won't do it), pay special attention to the last five pages. Understand those five pages thoroughly. What happens there? What are the metaphors? What's the subtext? What categories of human experience are plumbed there? Once you have a working knowledge of the end, start looking for threads of meaning that carry through the play and connect with it. Look for vocabulary that's present at the finish and also elsewhere. If in your opinion they are alienated in the final scene, go back and look for the contributing factors. You know what the treasure is; now go back and look for the bread crumbs that lead you there. Those trains of thought and action are the important moments of the earlier scenes. Remember also that you want to make those final moments special. If you rage at the end, don't rage in the middle. If you stand on the piano bench at the climactic moment, stay off it earlier. The last thing we want—the last thing to be—is repetitive.

INNER MONOLOGUE

You'll find a dozen definitions of this from a dozen teachers. Let's make it really simple. This is what you think while you talk. This means keeping your mind onstage and in the situation. It is a composite of backstory, acknowledgment, circumstances, actions, tactics and picking up what the other character is giving you. Some people actually write out their inner monologue for their scenes, but I feel that simply ties you down to a second text. Better, I think, to have done the homework implied by the vocabulary above, and let this lake of information exist in you to draw from spontaneously as you play the scene. Your inner monologue needs to exist in the now, not in your memory. You need to take in the current moment and respond freely, but out of an examined background. Yes, I do think if you're having problems with a small, defined section, such as a specific beat, you might write the inner monologue (always done from the character's point of view) in hopes of unlocking the section's secrets. In the main, pursuing the action provides the monologue. And don't forget your character's simultaneous sense of the obstacle that accompanies his action. That doubles the inner monologue.

THE INSIDE

THE EMOTIONAL RESPONSIBILITY

One of the most dismaying moments for the actor is when you read the script and find out you've got to break down on page 44 and find out about your mother's death on page 67. Just knowing you have to provide big emotional moments can shut you down.

How do you prepare? There's that old favorite, substitution, where you use a deeply emotional memory from your own life (even if it has nothing to do with the play's situation) to trigger you at the key moment, or you can depend on a profound sense of the play's and character's circumstances to get you into the moment and imaginatively touch the emotional release button. Mainly, you have to free yourself from the idea of having to produce emotion. Your best recourse is the action. Focus on the action (what you want the other person to do, feel, or understand) and forget the emotion. If it comes, it comes; meanwhile you are fanatically focused on what the character wants and needs and whatever you do will be right. Remember that emotion is not the point, it's the by-product.

PASSIVE STATES

Yes, I know, there is a professional understanding that the best acting moves a passive state to an active one. However, let's examine for a moment the nature of this passive state. There is a substantial difference between not doing anything and preparing to do it. In acting, the useful passive state is one of using the moment to gather, prepare, and find the spiritual and physical balance to leap forward. States of constant activity tend to wear the audience out. Which is more dramatic—the swimmer who bounds up the tower to the high dive and forthwith leaps in the water, or the one who pauses at the edge of the board, needing the moment to vanquish fear, and, then prepared, dives? Look for those moments or sections where your character knows what she must do but needs time to generate the will to do it. There is immense activity in these moments even though they are quiet and still. One more thing, these moments open the door for that ancient but valuable theatrical device, suspense. Don't mistake a "gathering" state for a passive one.

Jon Jory

VULNERABILITY

The actor must be affected by the circumstances and story in which he finds himself. He must first allow and then foster that vulnerability. In life we fight to defend our emotional vulnerability—to batten it, hide it, keep it out of the line of fire for fear others will ridicule or exploit it. In acting, to be over defended in this way is brutally limiting and can make actors incapable of first-rate work and first-rate roles. You can't come to acting to hide; you must come to reveal. The hard part is that what must be and is revealed is often unattractive, weak, morally fragile, and deeply flawed. I know many fabulously talented people who simply cannot allow themselves to be seen in this light, and their work, with these faucets turned off, leaves us unaffected. You must open yourself to the role's journey and reveal your weakness and inability to deepen the flawed character. If you cannot, will you ever be more than workmanlike?

WRESTLING WITHIN

Some people live uncomplicated lives. They have clear goals, they pursue them sensibly, and then they achieve them. These people are not characters in plays. Characters also have goals, but they are conflicted, doubtful. They aren't sure how to go about it. They are continually reassessing their methods. The character second-guessing herself makes for wonderful acting opportunities. Look for the moments when the character is thinking, "I could do this or I could do that. If I do this, it might work out fabulously, but on the other hand it might really suck." The character's internal wrestling match about what to do and how to do it has, after all, given us *Romeo and Juliet*. Romeo, in the balcony scene, doesn't just set out to win Juliet and then win her. He worries he'll get killed by her relatives in the garden (even though he says the opposite). He worries she doesn't really love him. Should he propose? Maybe it's too soon? She questions his love—can even *he* be sure of it? Let's put it this way, Romeos who have absolutely no problem committing aren't very interesting Romeos.

33

YOUR LIFE AT YOUR FINGERTIPS

Your life is your main resource, so keep mining it. Having a hard time falling asleep? Impatient waiting in line to deposit your check? Trapped at a play so boring you could immolate yourself? Send the bucket down the well of your life. Usually you'll need a key word or image to start your time travel. Use hot button words like *anger, admiration, jealousy, longing*. Eagerly go on the journey your memory takes you. Investigate the circumstances and feelings that each word illicits. If you want an even more surprising but less-focused trip, use concrete nouns. Think of all the *chairs* you've sat in (no, I'm not crazy), the *barns*, the *grilled hamburgers*, and you will find yourself in parts of your life you haven't thought of in years. Your own life is your best acting tool. You need to know it so you can recall what is crucial for a certain role. Bring more of it back to a conscious level.

RELIVING

There is an actor's instinct to relive every piece of text that speaks about the past. We don't do it in life, and you shouldn't be overusing it onstage. Conduct this experiment for a day: Listen carefully to conversations and see how often there is real emotion-memory when the past is being referred to. A very small percentage of the time, right? Usually when we speak of our childhoods, we're not reliving them; we are bringing our experience to bear on a present problem. We are using the past illustratively not emotionally. Every once in a while, references to the past are emotional triggers—as are smells, images, tactile memory, and many other stimuli. But make sure the narrative demands it. Don't simply gild the memory with what you consider the requisite emotional tone. You don't necessarily have to sound sad because the line is about the death of a dog, or happy because you see a hummingbird. What's the character's present use of the past?

A Secret Life

Someone—I completely forget who—said that every character has a secret life, and the character without one remains a simple construct. Yes, you must fulfill the necessities of the role but don't neglect the moment when we understand the handmaiden longs to be the queen. A supportive wife or husband might still have fantasies of escape and dreams of glory. The nerd wants to tango; the bully wants to raise flowers. Choosing a secret life for the character needs to take into account the play's structure. Nora, in *A Doll's House*, needs to be independent to find her true self, but at the same time she may have a secret dream of being a rich and powerful matron in an admiring society. Sometimes characters want to make the secret life known, and sometimes they struggle to distance themselves from the need. What is the secret life your character lives in daydreams and behind closed doors? Is there a moment in the play that reveals it, or a moment when she struggles to repress it?

Pushing The Emotion

The actor recognizes that a given section of the text is "emotional," and while he doesn't inhabit said emotion, he is determined to provide it come hell or high water. He sobs loudly, beats the floor with his hands, shouts and rages and flings himself about. He is truly terrible. He doesn't believe it for a moment, but that doesn't stop him for a second. Stop worrying about the emotion. Cease. Desist. If the emotion isn't produced by the flow of the acting, the circumstances, your belief in the story, or some reference you find in your own life, don't provide a stem-winding alternative. Simply want what the character wants in the moment. Absolve yourself of the emotional responsibility. Forget what the script says you should do, as in: "He weeps, he tears his clothes, he eats the proscenium arch." Trust me, nothing is as unendurable as forced grand emotion. Better to do something simple and real. Don't cry, don't yell. Speak quietly and drop your wedding ring into her glass of water. Better to do nothing rather than the empty and large.

THE PRIMEVAL OOZE

All right, come clean, what are you afraid of in the role emotionally? You decided to be an actor so you're going to have to get down in the muck. Where's the role's untrammeled sexuality? Where's the horrifying loss? Where's the uncontrollable paranoia, the petty, demeaning fear, the unattractive rage, the completely debilitating loneliness, the blazing narcissism? Are you sanitizing the role because something in you doesn't want to go there? Are you sort of halfway raging, sort of halfway lusting? When the primal is demanded, it's no good doing the cut-rate version. Today's the day. Cut it loose, throw yourself into it, let it consume you. This is why there have to be actors in the society. Someone has to tell the stories of the dark, the embarrassing, the extreme, the unmoderated—and you have signed on to do it. Don't put it off; it only gets harder. Yes, there may be foolishness and excess involved, but there is also enlightenment and the unforgettable. Go for it.

SILLY

You're often silly. I'm often silly. What about the character you're playing? It's particularly striking when a "serious" character gets silly. Now, what silly are we talking about here? I'm talking about the silly we want to have recognized as silly. I'm talking about singing a song that would be absurd in the circumstance. I'm talking about doing the soft-shoe in the rare book library. I'm talking about the silly hat, the outrageous Russian accent, the absurd imitation, the crossed eyes, the goofy walk. This sort of silly is often self-aware and even self-criticizing. It's often born out of the generous instinct to provide a laugh for someone who needs one or the necessity of making up for taking yourself too seriously. It can also be the perfect vehicle for creating the moment that needs inappropriate behavior. Any uses for silly in the role you're doing? The more dignified the character, the more striking silly becomes.

TECHNIQUE

Having tried to understand the play's intent allows you to find the key moments that reveal that intent. Framing is the way you communicate those key moments to the audience. Framing is making sure you give them focus. A whole book could be devoted to framing. You can frame by making the moment stand out rhythmically, by using pauses, by changing tone, by working with a prop, by using space dynamically, by separating out words and even syllables, by sitting when you've been standing or standing when you've been sitting. Usually, framing implies some change. Going from fast to slow, for instance, just before or during the key moment. Remember, you are trying to separate that key moment out, to make it unlike any other, to have it be remembered because if it is it will bring the audience closer to the heart of the story. Watch the veteran actors frame the key moments and learn the dozens of techniques from them. Framing is the actor's tool of narrative and clarity.

CLAIMING THE SPACE

There are mysteries in acting, and this is one of them. Why is it that some actors and some performances do what we call "hold stage"? I personally think it's an absence of fear. When shards or splinters of your fear of the role, the play, and your adequacy are present ("I shouldn't really be up here, I know you're not going to be interested in me"), the audience senses that desperate edge and retreats from it. The actor's physical and emotional discomfort makes the audience uncomfortable as well. The actor who truly feels the right to be in the space claims the space. This right is based on pursuing simple, completeable tasks that result in the character fulfilling her needs. Do that, and you'll feel this complex of fears recede. Fail to do it, and you'll sweat. Oh, and make friends with the space, which is the frame for your endeavors. Come early and take it in visually and orally. Move through it. Feel the space by becoming part of its architecture. Sense it through your feet and your body. Become a comfortable part of its volume. Now pursue your character's task and the stage is yours.

NEUTRAL

Remember the moments when you've seen the play spin out of control into melodrama or the long sections where the audience is worn down and then out by constant intensity? This happens because the actor doesn't understand the concept of neutral. Allow me to describe it. The actor is in a rage but is worried he will become violent or say something he will regret. He pulls down into a clear, simple, almost uninflected tone. This is neutral. Neutral can be a warning that unless the other character behaves, big trouble is coming. It can be a sign that the character is exhausted by what is happening and can no longer function. It can be a sign of fighting for control or the character's realization that emotion won't help her get what she wants. Its functions are several. Neutral provides tonal change and variety after explosive or high energy beats or scenes. It is the perfect medium for clarity when the text's words themselves have an impact the actor doesn't need to add to. It can take and hold stage in the midst of noisy, indulgent interpretations. It's a palate cleanser.

DOING IT IN ONE

Most reactions and many moves take place within one-beat. How long is this one-beat? One second. This is the natural (or base-line) time for something to happen without interrupting or changing the flow of the scene. If it takes two beats or three beats or (very seldom) four beats, it's a big, fat *moment*. Getting out of the chair? Do it in one. Reacting to the line you've just heard? Do it in one. Making a punctuating gesture? Do it in one. If you take longer than this "one" and there's no big reason, then you are letting the scene get soggy or the moment become flaccid. Did I say everything should be done in one? No, I said a departure from "one" is making a very specific point. This idea keeps the work crisp and stays away from ill-considered pretensions. A waltz has a rhythm that provides a structure to depart from. So does a play. In one-beat, you should make the transition. In one-beat, change direction. One-beat. One-beat.

Balance

For reasons mysterious even to me, I was an amateur boxer for ten years. For my trouble, my nose was broken six times, but it did result in the following advice to the actor: Onstage seek a balance point for the body that will allow you to move quickly and decisively in any direction at any moment. The boxer is poised to throw a punch from any angle. The actor is poised to respond. Now to achieve this physical readiness, the boxer's feet are sixteen to twenty inches apart, but acting doesn't always allow that. It is the *sense* of this balance that is crucial. Your body should tell you that it could move right, left, backward, or forward without further adjustment. A marvelous thing about this sense of prepared balance is that it almost immediately deepens your concentration and drags you into the present moment, a state of being that any actor covets. When possible, the knees should be unlocked and the body relaxed but poised. We are then ready to respond to impulse and give it physical form. One of the nicest things for the actor is that it gives increased physical capacity without the broken nose.

Hands Over Your Head!

If I had, God help me, filmed all the acting classes I've taught and reviewed them, I think I would find that less than 1 percent of these young actors ever had their hands above their shoulders or below their knees. You're probably thinking I have finally gone over the edge, but we're talking about virgin gestural territory here. What this tells me is that culturally we absorb the information that nice people don't do such things, and whatever you're not supposed to do provides rich exploration for the actor. Almost every large part, and many small ones, embodies moments of wild feeling, desperate circumstances, or comic explosiveness. When those moments come, you may find a use for these places the hands and arms never go. What I suggest here is that you need to give your body permission to explore the wilder shores of its possibilities. Otherwise, you will be unwittingly trapped in the Miss Manners' school of socially acceptable gesture.

Focus I

The truism for the actor is that some moments have to be more important than others. The first problem is figuring out what those moments are. I would say they are those moments that embody the play's theme. The second problem is when you can identify the important moments, how do you make sure they "land" with the audience? How do you give them focus? I am tempted to say that focus is delivered at that moment when you stop doing one thing and start doing another. You have been sitting—you stand. That moment has focus. You've been speaking quickly—you speak slowly. That moment has focus. You've been damning up the emotion—you let it flow. That moment has focus. Now this moment of change has to feel appropriate to the audience both logically and emotionally within the context of the play. Some of the methods for conferring focus are the director's job, but (in case you hadn't noticed) directors are fallible, and the actor must be capable of identifying the key moment and delivering it. It is a crucial skill and a lifetime's work.

Taking Focus II

Focus is where you want them to look and what you want them to hear to give the text clarity and the story impact. Focus leads us through the play and delivers interpretation. When what you are doing needs the focus, how do you take it? You take focus rhythmically when, for instance, someone moving quickly becomes suddenly still. You could take it vocally with a sharp, slightly louder tone than the previous line or moving to a slower delivery. Focus could be had by rising suddenly from a chair. This and a hundred other choices pull the focus, but in the hands of the textually uninformed or taste deficient, it's a loaded pistol. Taking focus when you shouldn't can be very destructive of both sense and context. Remember, you can light a match, slam a door, examine a shiny object, go still, go fast, or eat a flower. But why, and when?

BREATHE

When you need to get into the moment, when you need to be really present for the other actors, when you need to actually think onstage—breathe. Forgetting to breathe has been shown by several studies to be a primary component of panic. And panic, need I say, is not helpful to the acting process. Breathing centers you, calms you, promotes attention and concentration, and prevents your nerves from turning you into a whirling dervish. I have a friend who says he is so beset by adrenaline onstage that he writes the word breathe between the thumb and forefinger of his left hand to remind himself while he's acting. When you're not breathing, you are entirely focused on yourself. You need regular breath to liberate you to be with the other actors. I'm not kidding. Make breathing a priority in your next rehearsal or performance, and notice the change in your work. For one thing you'll be less afraid of silence and the pause, because your breathing fills it.

ANCILLARY ACTION

Life often stops onstage. Actors suddenly find themselves with nothing to do and a lot to say. There they are standing several feet from the nearest piece of furniture, nothing in their hands, standing like sticks devoid of behavior. The inexperienced look panicked, and the experienced radiate an angry confidence in standing still and doing nothing. For God's sake, give that actor something simple to do while he talks! Let them tie their shoes, file their nails, look through their wallet, clean their glasses, scratch a stain off their cuff, drink a cup of coffee, pick up change off the rug, eat a roast pig—something. It is simply amazing how an actor freed from the stage version of sensory deprivation suddenly lights up and makes sense of the material. Find a small task such as taking a sliver out with a needle, and let the completion of that task inform the speech structurally, finishing when the final period falls. Don't just stand there.

THE MEANINGFUL OBJECT

A prop remains just a prop until it becomes a vehicle for your character's hopes, dreams, rage, and joy. Let's have that object in the play—the one you kiss in victory or throw against the wall in defeat. Finding the props that do these things for you and the play heightens and expands your performance; otherwise, it's all just dishware. Which object in this play reminds you of your greatest loss? Which makes you the saddest? What object would your character carry first from a burning house or most miss after a robbery? These props are characters for you and with them you have powerful relationships. These props ground you and make the moments. Do you have these props in the play you're doing? Is there something specific you need? Don't be afraid to ask. On the other hand, some props are useful to the character because they are absent. You always look for a certain toy in your childhood room, but it's long gone. Make your character's relationship to the play's things as rich as his relationship to the people. Give those things personal histories. Befriend them.

STAKES

We all know the admonition, "raise the stakes." We know it means that whatever you want in the scene, you can change the complexion of the event by simply wanting it more. For one thing, raising the stakes usually raises the intensity and, often, the energy. It can make a scene central to the event and the actors' work riveting. These three words, "raise the stakes," are, in almost any circumstance, good advice. No matter how com-

monplace and ubiquitous this advice is, it is often overlooked.
Go back to it in the work you're currently doing. Keep raising
the stakes until your inner monitor (or your Director) whispers
that you're working too hard, you're shrill or you're frantic. At
that point, you can always back off. Sometimes the very idea
reveals that you don't know what the stakes are, and you need
to define them before you can raise them. Ask yourself.

THE ENERGY-DEPRIVING OBSTACLE

Let's recap. The action is what you want the other person to do,
to feel, or to understand. The obstacles are what prevent your
from easily completing the action. Now, sometimes the obstacle
depletes the action's energy. For instance, the obstacle forces
you to talk very quietly (the bad guy is only ten feet away), and
this seems to suck the energy out of the scene. You can restore
the dramatic drive by increasing the urgency. What you say is
quiet, yes, but the need in your void is powerful and palpable,
which keeps the text theatrical. Urgency is most easily applied
as a reaction to time pressure. You must achieve the action in
five minutes or die the death of ten thousand cuts. When the
obstacle seems to make the scene founder, become placid, flaccid, or passive, look for a circumstance that demands urgency
and then redouble yours.

SIX MOMENTS

Common sense leads us to believe that there are a finite number
of big moments in the role you're doing. These are central life-
changing or threatening moments for the character. If you play
too many, we may feel there aren't any. Too many and the role
flattens out, for all your passionate emphasis. Let's say (just to
choose a small number) that there are six. All right, what are
they? Tell me? You need to discover them, understand why they
are central, and then deliver them within the context of the play
in a way that makes them stand out. Your understanding of which
moments and how many may change as you rehearse, but unless

you target them the audience may leave without having understood you or the play. These moments highlight the play's story and your character's place in it. Very often there are too many rather than too few. Once you have basically worked through the text for sense and situation, take a pass through and think about the six moments. A small role may have one.

All right folks, the scene may not be playing because the vocal energy is too low. Everything else is copacetic. The action is clear; the obstacle is established. You're concentrating. The problem is that the lack of vocal energy is sapping the rest of your energy. This is where the very old-fashioned and somehow tackily British "speak up" can work wonders. To speak up takes an increase of energy. That increase, almost by itself, seems to heighten the stakes of what is currently playing. At the same time, this new energy radiates to all parts of the body and you feel impulses to move and *do*. The new drive to *do* naturally focuses you on "do what" and "how come"—thus refocusing you on the action. This forces the other actor to relate, and in a trice, everything's getting better simply because you spoke up. Its other virtue is that, to start with, it's not complicated emotionally or physically to do what's requested. Last step! Don't wait for others; request it of yourself.

THE NEEDS OF OTHERS

Don't be the solipsistic actor. Act for the other characters, not yourself. The complete actor studies the other actors' and characters' needs as well as her own. Your character and line are there to serve and provoke the next reaction. The classic example is having to say, "Stop shouting," when the other actor isn't. If your stage husband says he's leaving you because of your sarcasm, you might want to make sure you provide some. The dreaded (and often unethical) words from our scene partner are, "You're not giving me what I need." Figuring out what the other actor needs and making sure to provide it is "the setup." Actors expert at the setup work more often than others because they are recommended by other actors. Spend an evening enumerating the ways your character needs to set up the other characters. It's time well spent.

I KNOW THE LINE—WHAT'S THE ATTITUDE?

The line is, "Hey, great hair day!" Is the character's attitude toward the line he is saying complimentary, ironic, provocative, hostile or seductive? This ties in with the action and the tactic employed, but even the tactic may not always reveal the attitude. You may wish to convince your grandfather to go to the hospital but have an ironic attitude toward doctors and medicine in general. The attitude is how your character feels about what they are saying. Very often I hear actors delivering the sense of the line without providing an attitude toward the line, and the result is that wonderful nuances of character are lost. Very often, attitude is the iceberg tip of backstory. When you use the word "school," you are not only conveying information but opening the door on your character's years of experience in that setting. Sometimes a character is repressing an attitude toward what they are saying to gain a particular end, but this sense of repressing is what gives the moment its particular tone. "I know the line," the director says, "but what's the attitude?"

FINISHING

We can improve our acting by knowing and showing when something is over. Let's start with the punctuation, specifically the period. Yes, there are such moments as blending two sentences, but usually we need to bring something to a halt at the period. This also implies that we start something new with the next sentence. We have to *hear* the finish and recognize the new start. Beyond the period, there's another world of endings. There's the moment when you've made your point or listened as long as you can stand it. There's the time when there's no use continuing as before. The instant when you demand a change of subject, you need to be aware of the finish and act it. In life when the meeting's over, we often rise to signify it. Signaling to the audience when something is over is part of your job. Finishing is often important to the character as a sign of power or control. Be decisive. Provide closure. To stop is an active choice. Stop.

THE BUILD

The build is an essential building block of an actor's technique. It's centered on the moments (usually four to six lines) where neither party wants to allow the other to have the last word or end up "on top." Here's an obvious example: "Don't tell me that's what you meant." "I am telling you that." "How can you possibly believe that?" "Because it happens to be the truth." "It happens to be your truth!" "Enough!!" In a build, each line is louder than the preceding one. If there are five lines, there are five steps in the total build. The line at the top of the build caps it and provides closure. Builds are usually followed by a pause—short or long—depending on the emotions involved. The end of the build is very often the end of the beat. Ordinarily, the build is not more than six lines, but there are, of course, exceptions. Some builds you will find intuitively, some you will have to be looking for. The build energizes the scene and sets the stage for transitions to quieter moments. Do they appear on your radar?

ILLUSTRATION

Be careful not to illustrate the line. If for instance the speech is "I saw the big cat crouch and then spring forward, loping across the scrub brush toward the tall pines," it's probably not necessary for you to literally crouch, spring, and lope, or describe with gesture the difference between a tall and a short pine. The audience understood all that from the language. Acting it out would be, as one of my favorite character actors used to say, "too much of a muchness." There are, of course, moments when the actor glares balefully while he speaks of a baleful glare, but not, let us hope, too damned often. This illustrated form of acting lacks mystery and psychology. Remember that the tension between what the actor thinks and what she says is crucial. Illustration innately talks down to the audience creating the embarrassing sense that if you didn't act a muskrat when you said "muskrat," they just wouldn't get it. Have mercy! Can be funny in comedy though.

CLEAN

"He does nice, clean work." "The direction is so clean." "We need to clean this up." What is this clean? It usually means that only what needs to be there is there. If it's a gesture, it's sharp and defined with a definite beginning and end. The gesture isn't background; it's there to clearly punctuate and clarify the speech. If it's a piece of business, it has the same qualities. The door is opened briskly. The actor leans sharply out, looks crisply to his left, pulls back inside in a single motion and slams the door solidly. The qualities of clean are:

1. Completely in control.
2. Crisp, sharp, neat and defined.
3. Points made confidently, visibly, and without quirks or crotchets.
4. We see when something starts and when it stops.
5. Whatever is there is there to make a point—no more, no less.
6. It is precise in the way an athletic move is precise, and thus aesthetic.

So, that's clean. It's not everything, but you need the skills. It's basic.

PAPER TOWELS

Actors are continually running out of things to do: "I drank the coffee and put the cup in the sink, now what can I do?" Well, break what's available down into its component parts (remember we spend weeks without the real props). Let's say you spill spaghetti sauce on the floor and you want to clean it up.

1. Look for and get the roll of paper towels.
2. Take it out of the wrapper.
3. Open the door to the garbage.
4. Throw the wrapper in the garbage.
5. Rip off two sets of three towels each.
6. Put one set on the table.
7. Get down and wipe up the spaghetti sauce.
8. Throw first towels in the garbage.
9. Further clean with second set of towels.
10. Throw away.
11. Put the roll back in the cabinet.
12. Sit down.

And this is all done while talking. See, there was plenty to do. You just hadn't broken it down.

GOING BUT NOT KNOWING

OK, everybody knows (and everybody says) the great trick is to perform as if you didn't know what was going to happen next. Simple enough, but you do know. So, how to proceed. Look at it this way: You've got to work on the problems of the present and stay out of the future. You have a current goal (the action). She says a line. Does what she say get you closer or put you further away from what you're trying to achieve? React to the positive or negative nature of her lines. It is your current reaction based only on current information that keeps you in the moment. If you're still projecting, try slowing down. If you give yourself time to perceive the present, you are more likely to act in it. Also, check to see if right this instant (not at the end of the scene), you have something to lose. The current danger keeps you current. You stay in the present by pursuing the present need, even if it's not as dramatic as the crisis ten pages on. It's when the present moment doesn't seem to have interesting acting possibilities that you tend to play the future—which, remember, only the tarot cards know.

LOUD ENOUGH

Strangely, we need to talk about this. Everyone agrees they need to be heard, but in the heat of battle even the most experienced will sacrifice this necessity on some other acting altar. The basic conflict is between a realistic, conversational tone and "loud enough." As the size of the auditorium increases, the conflict heightens and the actor begins to find the necessary vocal level disturbs his sense of truth and concentration. Usually, the phrase, "It feels like I'm shouting," is next on the agenda. You're not shouting, but for the first time you're aware of your own sound production. At this point, you can probably reduce the decibel level if you increase articulation and slow down slightly. One piece of advice, do not rehearse for too long at a level significantly below the level you'll need in the actual auditorium. If you do, when you make the transition to the stage and start pushing the sound out you will feel, unnecessarily, that you have lost everything you had in the rehearsal room.

STANDARD AMERICAN PACE

And now the sort of heretical statement that can get you burned at the theatrical stake. I believe there is such a thing as Standard American Pace, and if we were aware of it and used it as a benchmark to depart from, we could solve a good many rehearsal problems straight away. Here's the deal: Standard American Pace consists of the following: line, one beat, line, one beat, line, one beat. The demand of this format generates an immediately sufficient stage energy. Using this as a basis, you vary it rhythmically as the psychology and complexity demands. When the text and the actor are in full cry, you pick up the cue directly off the last word. Need more time for thought, take two beats. Anything above two beats right on up to an endless fifteen is used to make points. Put it this way, if you don't have something important to do with the silence, you don't get more than two beats. Let's call this a workable oversimplification. It's how most American productions work and how their rhythms deliver content.

DETAILS: THE HEART OF ACTING

A man enters a room; he automatically reaches for the light switch he knows is there. He goes to the refrigerator, opens it, takes out a beer, then puts it back. He closes the refrigerator door and idly wipes a smudge off the handle. He smiles thinking how often his wife has asked him to do that. He remembers to take off his shoes because they are muddy, and then puts the ends of the laces inside because it's neater. These are acting details. There would be details of a different sort if he were speaking: interesting turns in the thought process, surprising emphasis, a clear understanding of who he was talking to and for what purpose. The telling details of thought and action are the difference between the good actor and the average actor. As they say, the devil is in the details, but developing details that reveal the character and the script is hard, laborious, careful work. Do it or be damned.

CONFIDENT ACTOR: HANDS AT SIDES

Ah yes, sometimes a good acting idea becomes so prevalent in American theater training that it lives on to become an unbearable cliché. In the sixties, with realism in the saddle and all forms of behavior transmogrified into eccentric physical tics, we all longed for actors who stood still, commanded the stage, kept their hands at their sides, and made their points without being fussy. Well, careful what you wish for. We got them—now our stages are littered with steely-eyed, confident actors commanding the stage without moving a muscle. It's sort of like Madame Tussaud's. Remember, there are moments that electrify because of their tense, coiled stillness, but most of the time we're brushing taco chips off our pants, going through our pockets for our keys, cleaning our glasses, or tapping out songs on our chests. You have to be careful that standing still with your hands at your sides doesn't read as being petrified of acting and not knowing what to do with yourself.

THE NEW PLAY

Is there any difference to the actor in doing a new play? If the playwright is present, yes. First of all, it's your job to say the lines as they are written—don't do your usual paraphrasing. Next, don't "playwright." This means it isn't your job to tell them how the story should change or what the resolution of your character should be. Don't say, "My character wouldn't say this." The playwright's character would and did. Finally, don't tell them your character doesn't have "closure"; he probably doesn't need it. On the other hand, feel free to say, "Could you tell me a little about this scene," or "Could you tell me a little about this relationship," or "Can you tell me a little about her background," or "Can you tell me a little about this moment." In the main, playwrights are interested in an actor's questions and not as interested in their statements. If possible, try to talk to the playwright before you go into rehearsal, but be careful not to bully the director with what was said.

ARTICULATION

American voice teachers' techniques and applications have

become increasingly sophisticated, but down in the actors' trenches, the simplest thing of all is still a problem. Articulation. It almost seems that the actor is taught so many things to concentrate on—from actions, to obstacles, to circumstances, to philosophies of space, to spinal alignment—that he often forgets to move his lips and deliver the words as if their arrival in the audience's ear were crucial. Let me say this twice for emphasis. The actor's major responsibility is to deliver the text. Once more, the actor's major responsibility is to deliver the text. Nothing else the actor does can compensate for failing this responsibility. And text delivery primarily depends on the consonants. Bite them, explode them, concentrate on them until it becomes second nature. Physical theater may be on the rise, but the text retains its primacy. Articulation.

OVERUSE

Actors do a hundred things, but they usually have one or two things that have been winners in the past that they do ad infinitum. What's your version? This actor who cries easily, cries all the time. This actor who gets laughs when he laughs, laughs a dozen times in every production. This actor (male and female) fetchingly shakes her golden curls. That actor slaps his thigh for emphasis. (Who have you ever seen slap his thigh in real life?) This actor invariably climbs up on the furniture. That actor endlessly chops the air in the same way for emphasis. These sometimes shrewdly habitual patterns can be useful if you change cities with every production, but in most cases, the audience is beginning to recognize them as belonging to the actor not the text or psychology. Often, as in selective forgetting, the actor doesn't know she's doing it. Sometimes the actor does it because he knows the audience will laugh or gasp (Olivier showed nothing but the whites of his eyes in several productions). Careful, they're on to you.

ATTACKING THE LINE

There are moments when we go from silence to speech that take care of themselves. These are usually moments when the story is carrying us, when the situation is so intense or so surprising that the audience leans forward to catch the slightest whisper. These aren't the majority of moments, however. Most of the time the actor has to attack the top of the line, enlivening it with a dollop of extra energy. Why? First, you need to take back the focus after the other actor speaks. Second, if what the other actor says doesn't energize you, why should it engage the audience? Some actors become death-ray energy drains, always sliding into their line under the level of the line before. There needs to be a steadily reinvigorated vocal energy to keep the text aloft and functioning. Acting is, by definition, not passive work, and most actors in most situations must demand our attention with the first three or four words of the sentence. Attack!

PACE

The basics of pace relate to information and emotion. Emotion can drive us forward, increasing speed or need to be controlled, slowing us down. Information must be delivered at a speed that allows it to be understood. Simple information might move quickly, complex information more slowly. A strong action can hurry us along; a strong obstacle can back us off. Stage speed (the rate of words per minute) is usually a tad slower than we speak in life, because in real life we can always be asked to repeat it. Given the fact that you could fix a section either by going faster or slower, I find it generally the case that most deliveries are too slow, too careful, and too many points are being made. Pace can only be laid on top of the actor's intent. Pace without content is a horror. Once the action is clear, you can try moving forward more quickly to make the audience sit forward and work ever so slightly to catch up. When driving the pace, remember the God "variety." There is no fast without slow.

BUYING THE PAUSE

Think of the substantial pause as surcease. Something important has been happening quickly or loudly, and now the need to think or the need to feel interrupts that rhythm or that sound. We buy the pause with forceful rhythm or sound that is then interrupted by silence and time. A pause usually breaks an established rhythm. If the pause is accompanied by a physical stillness, you can buy that stillness with strong activity beforehand. The pause is an acting garnish. It is rarer than sound. It is meant to signify. You must prepare the way for it. You must buy it with what you do in the moments leading up to it. Too many pauses equal too many points, and too many points make it hard to follow the narrative and/or the argument. Once you buy the pause, commit to it; don't simply indicate it. The pause should be completely used up, the necessary thinking done and the overwhelming emotion spent.

FINISH THE BROKEN LINE

"So James," I say, "when the character says, 'Listen, I . .' what's the rest of the line?" James stares at me sullenly and replies coolly, "He cuts me off at that point." "Yes, James, we know that, but if he didn't cut you off, what would you have said?" The silence is long. The reason you must know what the cut line is, is that otherwise it will be clear as day to both the audience and the other actor that you're faking it (truly, it's one of the most obvious frauds in acting). This fraud breaks everyone's sense of belief not only in your work but in the story. *Continue the cut line* until the other actor interrupts you. If he hasn't been interrupting you, your keeping trucking will instruct him. If the other actor has difficulty cutting you, give him a split second at the end of the written section while you "think." This allows you a sense of continuance and gives him a small window to pick up the text.

OVERLAPPING

There's something wonderfully life-like and real about two

people who speak simultaneously. It gives verisimilitude, picks up the pace and often seems to indicate that the stakes are high. It does, of course, demand agreement from both actors because overlapping someone else's line without their consent may put the rehearsal atmosphere on the boil. Two great American actors of the 30s and 40s, Alfred Lunt and Lynn Fontane (they were married and thus had extra time to practice), made an art of overlapping their speeches. They were so sophisticated with the technique that, while they were overlapping, one would pull down vocally for a few seconds so some key phrase in the other's speech could pop out, and then a split second later the other would return the favor. While this technique adds a dash of spontaneity, it is most often used when the last three or four words of a speech aren't crucial, and they can be lost without harm. Also, don't overdo it. A little goes a long way.

UPSTAGED

Ah, a nostalgic tip! Nobody talks about being upstaged anymore. It's become the stage crime that dare not speak its name. Just for the record, when you're acting on a proscenium stage (they still exist, drat their horizontal little natures) and the other actor is constantly anywhere from a step to a league closer to the set than you are, it forces you to turn up to play with her and the audience can't see your face. These days the crime is committed more subtly than in the past. Last week I watched a two-character play, and one actor was invariably six inches upstage of the other all night long. What to do when you're locked in battle with one of these stage thieves? Simple. Turn front. If necessary, turn front and move downstage. Play with the other actor verbally—but face the audience. You'll get the focus you need, and that bad girl (or boy) will shortly have to move down on your level to make contact with you. Do this enough, and the other actor will get the idea and share.

POSTURE

Why has posture ever been an issue? Why did your parents care? It's the aesthetics. Good posture makes the body look better in space. Bad posture is a character choice; good posture is the benchmark. Why do you never see bad posture in dance? Because nobody wants to look at it. Cultural ideas of beauty and line are theatrical issues as well. It may not be politically correct, but it's a fact. Good posture also has the virtue of being a prepared state. From its balance points, you can move quickly and efficiently in several directions. On a certain level, people go into the theatre to be looked at and, if we wish to be looked at, we must know how to provide the pleasures of balance and line. Good posture gives a sense of event and respects the audience; depart from it only to make a point. When you are poised, ready, proud, you create the basis for the confidence you need to hold stage. Study portraiture. Make us want to look at you.

Thoughts Per Minute

The actor of genius registers more thoughts per minute than the good actor, who registers more thoughts per minute than the average actor, who registers way more thoughts per minute than the bad actor, who registers practically no thoughts per minute. The firelight quality of the mind onstage endlessly fascinates us. The character's active mind takes in information, processes information, and gives out information, and the way it moves from one to the other rivets us. For the character's mind to do this, you need to be steeped in the circumstances, applying an action, using tactics to achieve it, and being aware of what you're getting from the other actor based on the history and complexity of the relationship. Far too often the actor moves too little emotional and circumstantial information through the playing, and thus the audience has nothing to do but wait for the special effects. Your brain is the most theatrical event onstage.

The Visual Cue

When we pick up cues tightly, we are speaking directly off the final sound of the preceding line. We also pick up cues off visual moments, such as a physical reaction to what we've said. He says, "I know you're pregnant." She turns sharply to face him. He continues, "I've known for a couple of months." He picks up the line off the end of her turn in the same way he would pick it up off the end of her line. The cuing off the visual cue can be tight or loose depending on the needs of the scene. There may be a tight cuing sequence where two or three of the cues are visual. Further, the visual cue you take for your next line may come from what you do in the middle of one of your own speeches. The person giving the visual cue needs to remember that the physical action needs a clear end that can serve as a cue. When we describe moments or performances as "clean," we are referring in part to the crisp deliveries of visual cues. If we can't see the end of the move, we can't take it as a cue.

LOVE SCENES

Love onstage is, in the main, the lover's action of wanting the best for the other person in the given circumstances. Secondarily, it demands a focus on removing the obstacles that are preventing love's fruition. It is not the infuriating saccharine tone used to signal, in capitals, THE LOVE SCENE. Is there a desire for touch, a drive toward sexuality? Obviously, that should be a result of the above, not its primary focus. Remember the movies where you waited ninety minutes for the kiss? The audience, sensing the chemistry, roots for the solution to removing the obstacle, and it is on the obstacle that you, the actor, should keep your focus. The other quality crucial to *amore* onstage is appreciation of the other's qualities. Don't just love, love something she does. Do *not* endlessly signal the audience that you are romantically and sexually available. This usually results in behavior so bizarre the audience looks away in embarrassment. Now go ahead, love!

BRING THE BODY, DON'T ADD IT

If you watch, with great interest, actors and acting for a very long time, you can't help categorizing. There exists a large group of actors who during what one might call the "figuring out stage" of rehearsal, lasting up to two weeks, put their bodies on hold. The impulses that would otherwise animate them physically seem derailed or devoted entirely to their thoughts, their examinations. During this period, one might think they have directed their nervous systems to carry *no* impulses rather than risk the wrong ones. They cogitate like wax columns. Nothing moves. Later they warm up and begin to allow their bodies into the act, but they have already lost the opportunity to try it a dozen different ways. From the very beginning, allow any impulses you have to provide a physicality. A thought occurs to you, let it reach your torso, feet, and hands. It's never too early, and you can constantly revise and change. Bring that body!

THE TWO MINDS OF THE ACTOR

Great acting usually works on two contradictory levels simultaneously. On the one hand, we are in the role; we become the character in the situation. Using ourselves (but submerging ourselves), we play as if the situation is real. A second self, however, simultaneously calculates acting possibilities, "If she's doing that, then I have to change what I'm doing." "Wow, that's the first time I really ever heard that line. It's much more hostile than I imagined. I can't go on being affectionate." "I've been in this chair for three pages, when can I move?" This second self is always seeking acting possibilities and looks and listens for them. You pay attention to the other actor both within the confines of your character and as an actor saying, "Well, if he does that, I would have to do this." The actor is aware both of her belief in the situation and of the acting opportunities that are presented. This dual awareness is useful because we often become self-regarding as we inhabit character, and that second level helps us look outward.

VOICE CONSCIOUS

I always remember my actress mother's disapproving look when she would say, "He's one of those actors who listens to his own voice." You can recognize these performers, right? God willing, you're not one of them. They, like Narcissus, have fallen in love with their own tonalities and are often gardening their own pitch and resonance rather than playing the scene with you. These poor souls were probably overcomplimented by family and friends on their "lovely" voice, and now, sonorous as all get out, they are driving us mad. Concentrate on the action and stop listening to yourself! If you have a good voice, you are blessed, but be careful not to lean on it as a substitute for other acting virtues. When being chased by a tiger, you won't be concentrating on your basso profundo. In acting, you're always chasing the tiger or being chased. Deal with that and leave your voice alone.

PUNCTUATING WITH REACTIONS

Don't be an actor who shuts down his systems while someone else does a big speech. The other's big speech is there to have an impact on you, and minus that impact, the speech will seem marooned—the traditional voice crying in the wilderness. Not only do we need to see the impact of the speech on you, your reactions are crucial to the transitions in that speech. So, in the midst of this backyard oration, she says, "So I don't care what you think. This might have been your business ten years ago." By allowing your reaction to fall after the word *think*, where the period punctuates the moment, you create the transition needed so the actor speaking can move forward. The audience doesn't simply focus like a laser on the speaker. They *look* for the reaction. Think of yourself as assisting the punctuation of the big speech, even when it isn't yours. There are no monologues when others are onstage. The listener creates the duologue.

DO IT ANOTHER WAY

You're locked in. The part's nailed down. In a sense, you're doing it like a checklist. I do this, then I do this, and finally, this.

It's safe. You feel confident and in control, but the flip side is a certain hollowness, a mechanical tinge. You know what the action is, what the circumstances are. Trust yourself. Play a little. Keep the structure; change the moments. Kill that wonderful gesture you've built into the moment a dozen times in a row. Let go of that reading that's become pickled. Sit a line later. Add a new prop. Handle the phone differently. If the section is repeated three times, change the details of what you're doing three times. Often, a small change or two lures your creativity back from exile. Sometimes it's astounding: You change a locked-in gesture, and suddenly you feel alive and flooded with new ideas. The difference between focussing your concentration on finding a new way versus repeating your delivery is often the difference between fresh and stale. Unshackle yourself. You'll both survive and prosper!

TRYING THE TOP

We, being the conservative, guarded creatures we are, usually respond to what happens to us onstage in a very middling way. After all, it would be tasteless if we did "too much," eh? Let's break that pattern and see what happens if we go big. When your sister confides in you that she has shot her husband, don't simply cast a distracted glance at the ceiling, literally fall backward out of your chair onto the floor or swallow that rose you've been sniffing. Director gives you the thumbs down? Fine, small is always available. But remember, something ballsier, something wild and even absurd, may carry the day and take you to a new level. A word to the wise: I would wait to experiment until the middle of the rehearsal period when you're beginning to feel knowledgeable about the role. Then look at several key moments in the text that are connected to the play's emotional center and risk a larger, more extreme response. When you hit it wrong, you just size it back down. When you hit it right, it's astounding. Get out of the middle a little. You have nothing to lose.

GETTING TO THE GOOD PART

61

I was watching a performance the other night and I thought, "Oh dear, this poor fool thinks it's *all* the good part. Where's the part he simply has to get through to *get* to the good part?" You know how that goes. Here you are giving directions to your directionally challenged spouse. He knows how to get to the library, so you tell him that part quickly, without emphasis, rushing through it, and then slow down and emphasize the tricky part going over the bridge. Where, dear actor, is the part you rush through to get to the good part? If you don't rush through any of it, how will we know what *is* the good part? Actors tend to treat every sentence as if it was precious plutonium. Find the dross and treat it like dross so the gold will shine. Find the part of the text you can rush through so quickly that it's right on the edge of being impenetrable. These are the parts where you say, "I know you already know this, and it's so simple I'm almost embarrassed to be saying it, but you see it leads me to . . ." Go ahead, rush.

THE GIRL WITH THE FIXATED EYES

There they are, unavoidable, those eyes that never leave yours. You act, and they bore into you. My God, they don't even blink? Some actors seem to believe that eye contact is meant to be as eternal as death and taxes. It can drive you so crazy you're afraid to look at them. Simple as this seems, let's talk about it for a minute. Humans don't make constant eye contact (well maybe when they're trying to be seductive). Our eyes move away and then back, or on rare occasions, avoid consistently. Remember that *where* and *when* you look can be both character- and plot-defining. Your job is not simply the other actor's eyes. Looking away often provides the obstacle in the scene. Often it provokes blocking as in: I move around to the other side of the sofa in search of your eyes. Remember that withholding your eyes is as powerful as giving them. The moment you give after withholding can be powerful. Don't be the lock-eyed monster.

PLAYING THE ARENA STAGE

No, you don't have to spin like a Lazy Susan. However . . .

1. The principles of acting are all the same, you just have to find reasons to be seen by everyone.
2. When you look away from the other actor, simply find a point of concentration that allows people behind you to see you in profile.
3. Some reactions have to be carried all the way round in a circle.
4. People don't mind not seeing your face for a couple of minutes. After that, a slight adjustment of your chair or a piece of blocking can solve the problem.
5. It's your job, too, not just the director's.
6. Find circumstances that allow you to be more diverse in the space. Is Godzilla coming? Look behind you.
7. In comedy, you often need to "pan" your reaction to the laugh line. The best way is to justify a move on the reaction.

Mainly, simply stay aware of long sequences in one position. Duh.

THE STRAIGHT MAN

We all want to play the funniest or most emotional role, but who is setting up the belly laugh or the emotional breakdown? What if we're cast in that role? The straight man used to be an honored profession for both men and women. It is the theatrical equivalent of the person in volleyball who sets so the other person can spike. These parts, the straight parts, offer wonderful opportunities for careful analysis and complex playing. How, in comedy, should the laugh line be set up? Do you need to be aggressive and loud, so the joke can be delivered quietly and offhandedly? Or should it be the reverse? Should you be sitting or standing? Should you feed the line quickly or slowly? How should you react after the comic line to build the laugh? In drama, how precisely do you need to prepare the atmosphere for Lear's madness? What is your responsibility in fueling Medea's rage? The great roles remain dependent on first-rate work by the straight man. Remember, you are there to provide what's needed. What's needed?

WHO YOU TALKING TO, HAMLET?

Yes, the soliloquy needs context. The director, irritated with your constant questions, says testily, "You're talking to the audience." As if that solves the problem. Who comprises the audience? Are they the King's court? Are they all psychiatrists? Are they assumed to be friends or enemies? If they are simply "the audience" in all their divergent splendor, then what is it your character wants from them? I have heard reputable directors of Shakespeare brush off such questions by saying, "It was simply a device in Elizabethan theater." Yeah? And how does that help? Don't forget the simple maxim that you need to be talking for a specific reason in a specific context. Just "talking" isn't a solution and leaves the speech in limbo with declined impact. If you have a series of soliloquies or monologues directed to the audience, perhaps you could change their nature each time. This one I'm saying to fathers everywhere, and this one is definitely to Poseidon. Give these speeches a logic beyond simple presentation.

RELISH

Relish means to take keen or zestful pleasure. Zestful pleasure! Where's that in what you're feeling, Mr. Oedipus? After your best performances, audience members often say to you, "You really seemed to be having a good time!" In drama, they tend to remark on your intensity and profound belief in the situation. In comedy, they usually mean you played the absurdity of the situation with fanatic sincerity. The audience sees "relish" as the actor's pleasure in concentration and situation. It sees "zest" as the energy applied to the play's problems and story. It sees "pleasure" as the actor taking on the demands of the role as if there were nothing—*nothing*—she would rather be doing. See that actor playing for high stakes? Now that's relish! Yes, there are characters who have lost their zest, but when they carry a heavy load in the production, what sustains their energy? When people in tough situations are described as fighters, we identify with their zest for battle, their relish for the din and clangor. Find the character's relish; it's an audience favorite.

When you read the memoirs of the leading actors and directors of the theatrical generation holding sway between 1930 and 1960, they seem almost invariably miffed by the "younger generation" taking too many "pauses." Taking the inevitable generational warfare with a grain of salt, it's still worth considering (in actor training I find they take too few). The pause mainly falls into three categories: thinking, emphasis, and emotional blockage. Thinking pauses are usually brief; the emotional pause where feelings prevent speech occurs at key moments only. It's that pause for emphasis that can be overused. Let's say the line is: "Well, I know you're worried about your brother and there was a little accident, but he's all right. It's Louise who's hurt." You see immediately you could take at least four pauses for emphasis. Perhaps you should take only one. You choose where. It obviously depends on which piece of information is the key plot point, the most dramatic, the most psychologically crucial. The thirties generation knew endless pauses for emphasis made the speech incomprehensible. Remember, emphasis is strategic as well as intuitive.

THE DOUBLE TAKE

All right, I know you've been waiting for this, what precisely is a double take and how would I use it in *Hamlet*? Most of us think the double take exited with vaudeville, but here's what it's about—surprise and recognition. The double take is the sudden understanding that the situation just got extremely interesting. That means it's potentially a tool for *Oedipus* as well as *A Funny Thing Happened on the Way to the Forum*. The mechanics are these: Something intrudes on your attention while you're doing or thinking about something else. You assume it's less interesting than what you're doing, so you throw it a quick cursory glance and look back at your own work. Suddenly you realize the possible implications of what you've just seen and refocus on it with your full attention. If it's Groucho Marx leading a rhinoceros, it's comedy. If it's Hamlet realizing the slight movement behind the arras is Polonius, it's drama. Mechanics: Glance left (or right) quickly and look back to the original point; now look left again with sudden or full attention. Bingo. They'll be doing them in the first regional theater on Mars.

THE SCALD AND THE BANDAGE

I used to work in a pre-Starbucks coffee shop where the job demanded doing about three things at once. The net result was that I spilled boiling water on myself about once a day. Let's call that "the scald." As soon as I did it, I reached for the ice and applied it. That's obviously the "bandage." Look for those moments where something somebody else says or does metaphorically scalds you. Let yourself react as instantaneously and painfully as if you had been burned. Don't hold back the reaction and don't underplay it. Treat those words exactly as if they burned you. (Obviously we don't do this six times in the same play.) If the play and character is decently written, the next thing that character will do is apply some kind of bandage to the wound. Just thinking of the next speech (sometimes it's allowing yourself to get angry) as a bandage allows you to better understand the subtext. Find the scald, understand the bandage.

FRAMING THE IDEA

Speech is an idea made audible. The idea onstage may take the form of a declaration, a question, a suggestion, a defense, a reversal, and so on. The acting question, of course, is whether the idea has already been conceived and the speech is the result, or whether the idea hits literally the moment before and the speech is a first try at articulation. In other words, are you having an idea or developing an idea? Depending on your choice, the speech has a very different shape and feeling. The actor makes this choice over and over in the role. Such choices are constant and the result deeply defining. The choice is sometimes a result of study and sometimes intuitive and spontaneous. What isn't often understood is that the result of these choices is, in fact, a characterization, an outline of how this particular person gets and handles her ideas. I guess I'm saying you need to have an idea about the form of the ideas.

A RHYTHM THING

The focus goes where the rhythm changes. If you've been speaking quickly and suddenly speak slowly, the audience takes in this new "slow" with particular attention and interest. The same is true with a new "fast," "loud," or "soft." Remember that once a rhythm establishes itself, we are lulled by it, only to be startled awake when it changes. Naturally, this is only helpful when the point of change is important to narrative or character. Take a football offense. You establish the run to score with the pass. Rhythm creates a tension because the audience realizes it will be broken somewhere in some way, and it waits to see how. If you're loud for a while, you will make a big point with silence. Think about those moments you really want the audience to get, and then figure out how you might change the rhythm at that point. You can use rhythm to give focus. The real question is, focus to what?

THE LIFT

Alas, acting energy often runs downhill. The scene or speech starts with a burst but slowly settles into a lower metabolic rate. Sometimes the actors pick up this passive level from each other. Every once in a while we need to reset the energy at a higher level. That moment of reenergizing the scene I'll call "the lift." Now please remember this isn't a ploy to maintain manic energy. Enough manic energy, we all know, is more than enough. This is a recognition that at various times we need to reinvest in our commitment to push the acting out into the house. The time to lift is usually at the point of the new idea. Having finished one thing, we need to introduce the next with a little panache. Each actor monitors the scene to make sure it is being played at a level that engages the audience's attention. When it isn't, someone (you) must take the responsibility and lift.

THE OPENING-NIGHT SYNDROME

I went to my opening last night, and the amphetamine pusher who haunts openings had really done a job! The actors had decided that if the play had been good before, it was *really* going to be good for press and parents. The actors played at energy levels unimagined during rehearsals. They threw themselves at the play like diving birds at a window. It was infinitely louder and infinitely faster, accompanied by wild gesticulation, and general mayhem was employed by all. Gone were the rests and pauses, and all rhythm disappeared in the general blur. I sat horrified. Who were these demons? They were actors "doing it *better*." Moral: Play the show you had in rehearsal. Don't psyche yourself up to give one all-or-nothing performance. As a matter of fact, calm yourself down for the opening. Soothing tea, sounds of the ocean, books on Zen. Just say no to adrenaline. Please.

PLAYING DUMB

The character who doesn't get it is a comic tradition, a tragic flaw, and a dramatic obstacle. When you're cast in this way, how do you create limited understanding from the inside? Now, we all have a hard time absorbing certain kinds of information that others master easily. When it comes to computers and mathematics, I'm definitely dim. The key is simply treating what you are confronted with as extremely complicated. Treat directions to a nearby market as plans for a nuclear device. Don't play "I can't understand." Play "I'm striving to understand." A second technique is to place your concentration off the point. My thirteen-year-old daughter may not absorb the simplest requests while she is watching television. Add large sums in your head while others speak to you. The third possibility is that the character actively doesn't want to know or understand. She doesn't like or respect the information being given. Or, lastly, play that you don't speak the language. Remember, you still need to play an action. In this case, you may choose an action off the point. By misdirecting your action, you will have played dumb.

DIALECTS FREEDOM

Most dialects I hear onstage aren't very well done or congruent with others, and a dialect coach is often too expensive. I am, however, amazed by a side benefit. Actors using them are often freer physically, less self-conscious, and more nearly "someone else." Why? It almost seems that the part of their brain involved in moderating their speech forces them out of themselves. So, here's an eccentric tip. If you're really having trouble with a role early in the process, ask the director if you may play it in dialect for one rehearsal. It's a way of shaking yourself awake inside the skin of the role, a way to jump-start yourself. If a genial director allows you to experiment (no, you're not going to open with a dialect), what dialect should you use? Anything you're really comfortable with. Yes, others may laugh and that's fine, but you also may feel opened up to a character who before seemed a bad fit. Worth a try. Of course, you may dissolve the entire room in sardonic laughter.

THE BOLT

We see people walk out of the room, meander out of the room, hurry out of the room, slide unobtrusively out of the room, but don't forget *the* bolt out of the room. Or even into the room for that matter. It used to be an English phrase, remember? "Where's Harry?" "Sorry, he's bolted." Now bolting anywhere for anything might basically be described as purposeful panic You're in the kitchen eating grapes, and you suddenly remember you left the baby in the car a half hour ago when you unloaded the groceries. What do you do? You bolt. You're late for a crucial presentation. You hurry out to the bus stop, and then remember you've left your notes at home. You bolt back into the house. "The bolt" is obviously a high-stakes moment used for either dramatic or comic ends. It's explosive, it's sudden, it's purposeful and dramatic. Got a place for one?

PRECISION

Precision is an interesting acting tool. The question is when to use it. A woman enters, she tosses two books onto her desk, flips her keys neatly over the sofa into a basket on her coffee table, kicks her shoes off her feet into a closet ten feet away, looks at her watch, points at the phone, it rings, and she sits, saying hello and picking it up simultaneously. Is this acting or circus technique? Both. Audiences adore precise physicality and business. They eat it up. It's particularly apt in comedy and productions that are highly styled. It's less useful in realist drama, unless the precision is a character trait. Precision, however, takes the stage. It commands attention, and when used inappropriately, reeks of overstated technique. So, precision is used to reveal character or to flat out entertain as a gimmick. It has a mechanical heart, so don't use it when something else is the point. Someone once said that psychology prevents precision, but precision can also muddle psychology. Everything in its place.

EASY TALKING

Words come easily, flowingly, and comfortably to some people and to others, well, they don't. Vocabulary often slips our mind only to be plucked from the void at the last moment. Sometimes the words we have aren't the words we want. And then there are the moments when we just don't know what to say. I've seen plays where everyone seemed to say everything they meant exactly as they wished to say it. Boy, it wasn't any planet I'd ever lived on. Yes, some plays have easier talkers than others. Shaw for instance, but even the immortal Shakespeare would recognize the battle to say what you mean. This gap between intent and language provides the listener with insight into the character and creates important tension. Some talking's easy and some isn't. Is that apparent in the role you're playing? Don't become a glib disc jockey of the soul.

Movement Demonstrates Psychology

What physicality makes our state of mind visible? Does she sit so she won't attract attention? Does she refuse to sit at the head of the table because she fears responsibility? Does he go into the kitchen a dozen times to check the turkey because he's insecure? Does he move slowly to the door to show he doesn't care? Does he continually brush off his clothes because he fears he's unattractive? You get the point. How can the blocking and your behavior reveal feelings? Don't leave it all to the director; you probably know more about the character's internal life than she does. Spend an evening thinking about the character's fluid psychology as movement. As we all handle ourselves differently in space, the use of space reveals the mind and its preoccupations. Put your feelings in space and behavior. Acting is often mind and heart made visible.

Pointing Your Feet

A 19th century actor has been secretly implanted in our brains by a foreign power. This accounts for the fact that whether actors are on a proscenium, thrust or four-sided house, they tend to stand with the upstage foot pointing at the other actor and the downstage foot cocked toward the audience. This is, not that anyone would remember, called "opening up" and has single-handedly supported more chiropractors than college football. It is also understood by experienced audiences to mean that the actor isn't really in the scene, he is primarily concerned with being seen. Even actors who have no technique do this. It is not only pernicious but ubiquitous. By signaling your nervous system with this hoary habit that it's all just "acting," you increase your self-consciousness exponentially. Point both your feet toward the actor you are playing with and trust, if necessary, your profile. Your concentration and belief in the scene will more than make up for the sight lines.

PROP ACTING

There are actors who tell a story with the prop they're holding, and actors who simply hold the prop. Yes, we all did the exercises in acting school, but as time goes on we tend to forget the lesson. Props are symbols and metaphors as well as Pepsi cans. You can see a long relationship in the way a person cleans up a room. The way you crumple the love note tells us volumes. Examine the use of every prop you touch in this play. How can you invest this object with a meaning that moves the play forward? Once you pick up an object, there are a hundred ways to put it down. A few of them will tell us something the playwright wants us to know. Work with props takes focus, so make sure your character deserves it at the moment you twirl the chair on one leg. Not only how you handle the prop signifies, but how and when you pass it to another character. Often you need one to use during a big speech. If no prop is indicated or given, ask for what you want. Use the prop to tell the story.

SITTING

And now a tip from the last generation. The act of sitting down is not inherently dramatic, and yet we do it several times in every play we're in. We know it's an act of characterization . . . how your character sits. We know your character has an attitude toward it that depends on the situation and circumstances. We know that when you sit punctuates the speech. We know that sitting can be a metaphor that helps us understand something about our lives (no, I'm not kidding). But do we know how to sit? We want a method where we can maintain eye contact if we choose, look graceful if we wish, and punctuate an important moment for us, if need be. All right, move to the chair or sofa or barstool or ledge, feel the sitable with the back of your leg, and sit down in one easy movement without looking back, Stay in control the whole way—don't fall into the seat, and don't take more than two seconds to get there.

PUNCTUATION (PHYSICAL)

Gesture, most often, is punctuation clarifying text. So is sitting, standing, starting, stopping, entering, leaving, putting your Coke down and slamming your book closed. As a single instance, take sitting. Don't sit anytime; sit to close an idea. You're crossing right, turn back on the comma, and remove the tiara on the question mark. Behavior reveals character, but it also clarifies ideas and closes out beats. If a gesture doesn't characterize or punctuate, get rid of it. Yes, the stage direction says she closes her umbrella, but when? Closing your umbrella is an opportunity to punctuate a point. Too many lost opportunities for punctuation give the performance a soggy, amateur look—plus the text remains unserved. Period.

STILLNESS

Stillness is potential. Stillness is the signal that big things are on the way. We all quote "the calm before the storm," but in performance after performance, the actor forgets its wisdom and is constantly in motion, constantly fidgeting, constantly using excess energy to no good end. Review what you've been doing in the play. Where are the significant moments when you are poised to spring—every sense alert, feet under you balanced for action, unblinking, dynamically still? Couldn't you use another one in that scene? As in so many other opposites we make use of, there is no motion without stillness. Very, very often, these still moments frame and in fact deliver the physical explosion that makes it all not only clear but dramatic. Remember that when you are still, any movement reads. A nod, a foot sliding back, eyes closing—the small gesture seems large against the stillness.

THE LONG SURPRISING PAUSE

This is akin to that supremely dangerous and astounding moment in bullfighting when the toreador, in complete command, turns his back on the enraged bull and walks away. We're not just talking pauses here, we're talking about that defining moment in the text where the actor, poised before saying or doing that which will change his or her life, holds us in a silence that lasts what seems like a thousand tension-filled years. Well, maybe not that long, but perhaps ten seconds or longer. Let us not suppose these opportunities come along very often, perhaps once an evening in a serious play. They are situated at moments where the audience desperately hopes for one outcome but fears another. They are the moments of highest stakes when the actor wrestles mightily not to do the wrong thing or gathers her forces to do the impossibly difficult right thing. The moment rivets and amazes us because of its daring and rightness. Where's yours?

CUING

Just as music does, cuing has a beat. The normal pattern (from which we will often depart) is the cue, then one beat, then the line. Tight cuing picks the line up right off the final consonant of the cue, driven usually by strong actions and high stakes. Any interval longer than one beat is a pause and is there for a specific reason. A pause may last up to five seconds, with the occasional star pause (after your father tells you he's remarrying or the police discover your embezzlement) that might take up to ten. Energy-draining (and often sloppy) performances will take two beats after the cue, line after line, without understanding that they are indicating important points exist where they do not. Tight cuing keeps beats and narrative together so that a whole unit of thought can be understood as a whole. Loose cuing indicates there is a lot of complex thinking necessary before speech is possible. Sometimes cuing has not only to do with the narrative or the character's inner life but with varying rhythms to hold attention.

CURTAIN LINES

All good things come to an end, and if you're lucky you get to say the last line. Usually, though certainly not always, what you need to do with the final words is firmly and clearly to provide closure. Whatever the attitude and emotional quality of the moment, it needs to punctuate. It is the tragic or comedic period, not a comma. It doesn't hurt to take a moment before you say it, to put a little frame around it. It doesn't hurt to find a sound to go with it—the clink of putting down your glass, the scrape of pushing in a chair, the clunk of tossing a book to the floor. Also, the more emotional the moments before the final line, the more simply it can be delivered. The last words of *Long Day's Journey* are, "I fell in love with James Tyrone, and was so happy for a time." It obviously needs a pause to frame its finality. Where will you put it? And what will be your last physical move in the play? A sit? A lowering of your head? What?

ACTING WHILE THEY'RE TALKING

Sometimes I watch a performance and realize with a shock that the actor in question is only acting while she talks and becomes entirely neutral on other people's lines. My second shock, once I become aware of the phenomenon, was that I could usually find someone doing it in every play I saw! Given the fact that acting is reacting, it is a dreadful habit. The best acting exists not in Actor A or Actor B but in what happens between them. If we accept that the action is framed to affect the other actor, we realize keenly that if we cannot see and understand the reaction to the stimulus, the process breaks down. There are, of course, periods of time when the actor is completely concentrated on understanding what is said to him, or is attempting to mask his reaction for a reason, but in every case these are the lead-ins—usually brief—to visible reaction. Make sure that half your work is spent reactively. The power of that work is enormous.

LOUD AND SOFT

Loud is a garnish; so is soft. There is a basic tone for the stage which is that level where everyone in the theatre can hear you. Above that is loud—below that is soft. I've had actors tell me (often) that they feel like they are shouting when they are actually using the basic tone described above. Too much loud wears us out, and too much soft makes audiences angry that they've paid their money. Make sure, early on, that you establish clearly for yourself what the basic tone is for the house you'll be playing in. Because without that knowledge, soft and loud become useless tools, and you can't afford that. Ordinarily we don't rehearse in the playing space until late in the process (but how nice it would be!). That being the case, you need some time on the stage prior to dress rehearsals. Beg, borrow or steal. And I'm not talking about thirty seconds to run a vocal scale. You need fifteen minutes to a half hour to discover the basic tone necessary, and then, using the text itself, trying out the larger as well as more restrained sections.

THE HALF-HITCH

One of the problems when we are driving the pace has to do with the oppressive nature of constant sound. When cue after cue is picked up, it begins to seem less like words and meanings and more like white noise. So when the fast pace is necessary, provide a little variety with the half-hitch. Let's say that the line that precedes ours is, "So I've decided to sell the car," and you say, "I can't understand why you would do that." The half-hitch might work like this, you pick up the cue tightly and reply, "I can't . . . understand why you would do that." The pause is brief, a half-beat or a shallow breath. You could, depending on your sense of the line, put it anywhere in your speech and use it for a quick dollop of thinking time. It breaks the flow of sound. It allows you a sense of spontaneity and thought process, and yet there is still the sense of cue pick-up and things moving forward. Real speech seldom moves in a steady stream. Listen for the half-hitch in your own life.

Faster Or Slower

There are two ways to improve what you're doing: go much faster or much slower. Faster demands attention (we're talking words per minute here), because if the audience is interested they'll have to fight to keep up with you, which means they are engaged. Slower surprises and engages if it is below your culture's normal rate of speech. You can even draw out a key moment one-word-at-a-time. Now when was the last time you did that? Faster and slower are also interesting when attached to a surprising mood or revelation. I remember someone rata-tat-tatting out the information that she was bored, monumentally bored. Or someone emphasizing slowly I-am-the-fastest-100 -metre-runner-in-theworld. Faster and slower are obviously emotional entities tied to an evolving psychology. But you ought to try the opposite speed in a tough moment. It may be the solution. One thing—information provided at a slower rate than the viewer can absorb it, for any length of time, is death on wheels.

Throwing The Line Away

Most plays we see are literally dying from over-emphasis like a weed-choked garden (if they are dying from under-emphasis, it's even more disastrous, but at least it's quieter). Throwing the line away is almost a lost art. Why do it? To save the emphasis for whatever is central—to prevent too much shouting, ferocity and pounding on the table—to save melodrama for the melodrama—to give us some ease and grace. How do you throw a line away? By laying it out quickly, lightly and offhandedly. Clearly, yes, but without a lot of emphasis, and it may not be a single line but a whole speech or a series of speeches. There is the definite sense of the actor saving herself, keeping much in reserve. When do we throw a line away—before or after we have done or are about to do some high-powered acting—to provide the calm before the storm—to put focus on actions rather than words. Oh, and when throwing the line away, articulate even more clearly. The throwaway is still meant to be heard.

DROPPING THE END OF THE LINE

The American actor drops the vocal energy at the end of the line, and it's a serious problem. First of all, there's the simple difficulty of understanding. Secondly, the heart of the line is often at its end. Thirdly, it's an energy drain on the role, scene and play. Most importantly, it's destructive for the other actors. The cue is the springboard for the response. It's like the fastball down the middle for the hitter. It sets up the next moment and demands reaction. The cue is a provocation—clear, sharp, even aggressive. When the energy drops at the end of a line, it's like trying to pick up Jell-O with your bare hands if you're the actor responding. The responding actor should be able to undercut the cue or ride above it to make the point. The cue needs clear final consonants so it can be picked up immediately if need be. Listen to yourself.

LISTENING

Every acting teacher and director has given you the "You need to listen" note. But how? In what way? To what end?
- We listen for sense. What are the words?
- We listen for the action. What does this person want of me?
- As we listen, we agree, disagree or feel neutral. What's our

attitude toward what's being said?
- We listen so that we may react in the context of the actual tone and sense given, not what we've already decided on.
- We listen so we may decide what to do.

As it is true that acting is believing, it is likewise true that listening is reacting. If you are impassive, it is because there is a benefit to your character in being impassive. You can also play with attention and inattention once you understand the text. Real listening is a relaxed state out of which response and action arise. Actor fear, stress and worry can make us deaf.

RHYTHM

Rhythm on stage is composed of quick, medium, slow—plus loud, medium, soft—plus pauses of all lengths, and the way we come out of them. The way the playwright composes the line gives us a basis. Is it staccato? Is it languorous? Does it go long line, short line, long line? What do the emotions and actions driving the scene do to create the rhythm? As a dramatic necessity and device, rhythm often uses juxtaposition to call attention to key moments. Fast, faster, stop. The stop marks the moment. A jagged rhythm in the speeches can create tension and suspense. An interesting rhythm (obviously tied to meaning) gives the audience pleasure and holds the attention. Find rhythms even in the most realistic and behavior-driven texts. Rhythm has to vary more often than any but the very best of us realize. After three or four sentences, the rhythm begins to lull the auditor rather than grab them. Thinking about the rhythm needs to be part of your creative process. Talk is jazz.

DANCE AND MUSICAL SKILLS

How many times in non-musical plays (talent being roughly equal) have I cast the actor who waltzed proficiently because of a short sequence in Act II? Answer: lots and lots. If you want to work, you should waltz, fox-trot, tango, be able to do a time-step, and a little tap would really help. This is not for musicals; this is for plays. You have a little time and a few dollars? Well, hie thee to the dance studio and make up for this oversight in your youth. It will pay off with more casting, I guarantee you. And, while we're on the subject, what about your piano, guitar, fiddle and accordion lessons? An actor who can play an instrument middling well will find themselves getting a part they would otherwise have no chance for. The actor who wants to make a living in this profession needs these skills. If you put in the work to develop them, that wonderful moment in an audition when the director offhandedly asks, "You don't happen to tango and play accordion, do you," and as you see his eyes light up at your answer, it may be a turning point in your career.

TORQUE

Torque is the moment when energy explodes, whether it is physical or vocal. It's a slang term from the world of drag racing for the car that literally catapults from a standing start to full speed. In acting, it's when whatever you've been holding back, keeping the lid on, suddenly pops out like a jack-in-the- box. It's very like what happens when you flip a light switch. The light doesn't dim up, it's just there—full force—instantaneously. A lot of people don't have it in their own lives; it just isn't in their metabolism, but it needs to be an arrow in the actor's quiver. Something, a circumstance, a psychological trigger, sends a jolt of energy through the actor's body that results in a flash of words or activity that may (or may not) just as suddenly be gone. In the character, it's the end result of suppression, of holding back, of holding onto a rationality in irrational circumstances until . . . boom! But, once again, where does it happen?

PUT THE SCENE BETWEEN YOU

The scene doesn't exist in you, and it doesn't exist in your scene partner. It exists only between you, at that living center where action meets reaction, and both attitudes are transformed. The scene stays between you when whatever she says and however she says it colors your reply, and the color of your reply then colors her reaction. The scene splits when an actor in the quiet of his study has decided how he will say each line. This dissolves the unity of the scene because no matter what actor A does, actor B will respond in a predetermined manner. To keep the scene between you, you must have an action which is subtly adjusted each time the other actor speaks. To do this, you must be focused and open to the other. You must have the confidence that you know the situation and its circumstances and backstory so well that you can proceed spontaneously and still stay within the context of the scene. Your homework (text analysis) now pays off because you won't lose track of the situation while you are free to respond intuitively to what you are given. As in the tennis volley, each return takes into account the other actor's position while hoping to win the point.

KEEPING THE LID ON

The longer you resist the outpouring of emotion, the greater the fight for calm; the stronger the will toward rationality in the face of provocation, the stronger the head of steam; the higher the level of suspense, the more satisfying the final explosion. Usually, the impetus carries all before it too early. Release is such a satisfying moment for actor and audience that we don't want to give it without a little withholding (in fact, teasing). The audience hungers for the first touch in the love affair. Hold back on it. The audience sees the tension building toward violence. Make them wait. The marriage is moving toward argument. Don't go there too early. For the actor herself, this reining in allows real emotion to grow bit by bit and a belief in the situation to flower. We have happily read books where we waited 200 pages for a wedding proposal or a fight to the finish. We'll certainly wait till the end of the scene for whatever you have cooking. Are you giving up the good stuff too soon? Don't.

SELF-REACTING

You react to what others say, and you also need to react to what you say. You can find what you say funny; you can find you don't believe what you said. You can be amazed at your own wisdom, stupidity and overweening ego. The point here is not simply to say the line but to leave yourself open to feel its impact. We listen to ourselves as we speak. We search for the right word, we revise in mid-sentence because we have thought of something better. We take issue with ourselves because we hear our own logic as fallacious. When I watch an actor who never really hears what he says and fails to judge it in the context he said it, I am fairly sure there is no real thought process. This tool is particularly useful in the long speech which has its own developing logic and changing point of view. I must add, however (on behalf of the playwright), that self-reacting does not extend to adding dialogue to embody your reaction. No extra "Wow" or "But see" or other spontaneous outbursts, just changes of tone, speed and the judicious use of "thinking pauses."

DRAFTING

You hear about this in Formula One racing. Drivers swerve in behind a speeding vehicle and are, in effect, pulled along by the created draft. There is something rather like this in acting. Sometimes you are onstage with a whirlwind of an actor. The energy coming from his side of the stage would be enough to keep Chicago supplied with electricity. You don't need to match it. In fact, matching it would probably overwhelm the scene. The audience, at first taken with his manic energy, soon begins to look to you for a reaction. I'm not suggesting you undercut his work, but some balance can only help. Your work in such a circumstance needs to be clear and strong and controlled. You become the one in the scene with potential, with the capacity to surprise, the one holding back who may or may not reply in kind. In a sense, his release of energy becomes your setup. It is reminiscent of karate, where you use the other's forward movement to throw him. The way to take stage from shouting isn't to shout!

SETTING AND FREEZING

As a rule of thumb, I'd say that you should be trying new things,

82

changing and adjusting until, well, four or five days before you tech (assuming a four- week rehearsal period). This last period is for making final decisions and polishing. Two things will usually be going on in these final days. First, the director will be working "bits and pieces" throughout the text, spending ten minutes to half an hour cleaning up very small sections. Second, there will be daily run-throughs of at least an act. The actors usually "set" or "freeze" those sections that include complicated blocking, fights or moments when someone could be injured, dances, sections with distinct rhythms, difficulties with props, love scenes or other types of physical contact. This "setting" means it will be done the very same way (down to the details) in every subsequent rehearsal and performance. No fooling around. This same process might be applied to the physical forms of emotional moments so that they don't lurch out of control. The director may specifically state that sections of the play are more open to change and/or improvisation, but if it's not said, we must assume it to be "set." Most (but not all) professionals find actors who don't "set" to be colossal pains and potentially physically dangerous.

Agree / Not Agree / Neutral

On the simplest level, these are the three states of reaction. Someone says something to you and either you agree with them, you disagree with them, you're not sure, or you're not willing to show your feelings. The important thing here is to show (no matter how subtly) your agreement or disagreement on a moment-to-moment basis. It drives you into listening and reacting, which, after all, is the beating heart of acting. It also teaches you about the role and the scene. If you find yourself having a difficult time determining which of the three your reaction falls into in a given section, then probably you need to sit for a time in a quiet place and work it out for yourself. Additionally (and again, roughly), these categories can fuel your blocking instincts. I agree—you move toward or shift toward or lean toward. I disagree—you move away or shift away or lean away or look away. Neutral—stay put. Is this simplification? Indeed, but until your sense of the scene is too sophisticated for these categories, they will get you going. They will make you do!

FINDING THE LIGHT

A lot of the time when I'm directing, I'm saying (in the techs), "If you would come forward (or go back) two steps (or one), you'd find the light." Lighting designers love the actors who work with their light. It isn't always the simple act of being lit; sometimes you want the sidelight and sometimes the back light. During the pauses in tech when the actor has spare time, experiment with the light you'll be in. Look up above and try to see the special that's supposed to isolate you down left. Find the hot spot, the place from which the instrument looks the brightest. When working in the special, ask the designer if you're standing where they want you, or "Is there a way I can handle this special better." The actor who works in tandem with the lighting designer to get the desired "look" becomes a favorite with the crew and often (don't tell) gets special treatment that heightens that key speech you love.

WEARING CLOTHES

Frankly, we're talking here about making the costume part of the characterization and (don't tell anyone I said this) showing the costume off. Costumes have a vocabulary of movement and even sounds they can make. They swish, they twirl, they glide, and they can be thrown back, opened, closed and draped rakishly over the backs of chairs. They provide fabulous hints about character and can be used to tell a behavioral story in the same way a prop can. When you've had a fitting or two, sit quietly and itemize what your costume can do and when in the script it would be useful to do that. If style or elegance is a useful concern, you'll want to know how best to sit, stand, lean and lie. Unsure—ask for advice from the designer. One more thing: If you are wearing a beautiful 18th century gown on a proscenium stage, find a reason to turn around and show the audience the back. There are dozens of hours of stitching, draping and designing back there, and it's your job to show it off.

STONE HANDS

Not all people, and certainly not all actors, know how to touch, how to communicate positively through the laying on of hands. I see actors take another's hand as if they were attempting to crush a hamster. The pat on the back is done clumsily and harshly, thus the term "stone hands." One of the most disconcerting and belief-destroying experiences for the actor onstage is to be touched in ways that destroy the intimacy the touch is supposed to engender. In life, we run from these people; in theatre, we have to endure their touch nightly. Your touch (fight choreography aside) is meant to be pleasant, reassuring, tasteful and affirming. If all we feel is the person's nervous state, fear of touching, and alienation, our belief in the scene crashes and burns. Commit to the touch. Make the touch communicate the action. Remove from the touch gently, not abruptly, and the concentration on the stage and in the audience increases. No stone hands.

DIRTY IT UP

A stage compliment: "Her work is so clean." This means there is nothing there that doesn't need to be there, nothing but the necessary, evocative gesture, the clean sit, the unadorned cross, no fidgeting. Well and good, but sometimes the geometry of the blocking, the figure standing in space with her hands at her sides, the sharp look away and then back has the feeling of machinery rather than humanity. Sometimes it is all too clean, too heavy a gloss of technique, too cocky by half. The blocking, all angles, needs the breath of life that vacillation gives. "I'm going there. Oh, no, I'm not. Yes, well I will, after all. Well, maybe not." The clean confident line of the actor showing us he doesn't even need to gesture while he does the big speech is somehow a statement about actor's ego and puts us off rather than drawing us in. It is then that we need to "dirty it up" a little. Add a touch of insecurity, a random scratching, a little bad posture, a little hesitation that breaks the efficient geometry of the blocking. It needs our humanity.

REPETITION

I am in tune with the great English actor Ralph Richardson's offhand remark that, "Repetition is the soul of art." Repetition eventually frees us from our concentration on the mechanics of acting and allows us to think freely within a fairly rigid form. The actor is thinking about the blocking, the props, the action, the obstacle, reacting to the other actor, so how can they be freed to inhabit the form of the role spontaneously? Repetition. As a director (and as a producer watching dozens of other directors' work), I've noticed that in going back over a scene or section, it is most often repeated twice, and occasionally three times. At that point, everyone's bored or frustrated and wants to move on. I want to suggest four as the magic number in repetition. When I have been able to force my unwilling psyche into four repetitions, I have seen a measurable increase in concentration, openness and discovery the fourth time. Some sort of fear and constraint drops away; props and furniture, and even our own bodies become our friends rather than our obstacles. Try it.

MAKING FACES

My father, an actor, used to answer inquiries concerning his profession by saying he "made faces for a living," and so in actuality he did. And so do you. Very often, after a long, complex discussion of action, obstacle, metaphor, theme and God-knows-what, I'm driven to say, "So, you agree that this is the fulcrum moment when you understand he's trying to steal your rhinoceros." And if the actor says yes, I will actually reply, "Then make a face!" All too often we know that what we are playing in a situation we could exhaustively describe, but the audience will never know. Internal process is the single distinguishing feature of the fine actor, but internal process that shows. I suppose in the cause of good taste, we should say, "Make half a face," because usually what's wanted is a blink of understanding, the infinitesimal nod, and the ironic gleam in a sidelong glance. Remember too that the other actor works off what they can see in you, not what they can intuit.

SIMPLIFY

The eternal question is always "can you do less and achieve the same effect." The answer is "sometimes yes and sometimes no," but you must ask the question. The aesthetic value of simplicity and austerity lies in focus (it's easy to see one red dot on a black background), in clarity, and in the elegance of the perfect single gesture. Simplicity, if it still reveals and expresses the text, has explosive impact. In the third week of rehearsal, it assists to spend a couple of days seeing what you can cut away without harming the structure you have built. Do you have to slam your fist on the table three times; wouldn't once be enough? "Wouldn't once be enough" is an excellent question to ask of your own work when you are close to finalizing the performance. Excess can be valuable in early rehearsals; it gives you a broad palette to choose from. In the end, however, excess damages focus and simplicity asserts it.

WORKING TOO HARD

Energy is the delivery system for meaning. More energy than the task or the scene requires is a failure of taste. Calm down. Save the demonic energy for a key scene or a key moment. When the director tells you (or should) that you're "working too hard," she means it's been too loud, too fast and too busy for too long. Many actors cannot disentangle speed from force. Very often, what's needed is light and quick, not quick and pushy. A basic giveaway is shrill. When your sound becomes shrill, you're working too hard. A little shouting or flailing goes a long way. Ask the most experienced actor in the play if you're working too hard; they very often know better than the director who mistakes your excesses for a good way to get through the boring parts. Your best tool to avoid this dangerous state is variety. Three lines of loud need soft. Three lines of quick need slow. A big dose of movement needs still. Or change your tactics.

SCARING PEOPLE

One of the great pleasures in the theatre is to be frightened. When it's your responsibility to frighten, what are your tools? We, as audience, usually experience fright when we know something will be said or done and don't want to see it or hear it. Count Dracula scares the bejabbers out of us because we know his potential, and yet he is courteous and quiet and still. We wait for the monster to emerge, but the monster keeps us waiting. It isn't the pistol that frightens us, it's waiting for its concussive sound. The scariest moments on film are usually preceded by a close-up of the eyes. It is the potential we see there that raises the hair at the back of the neck. One moment of rage early lets us know it's in there waiting, that the weapon is cocked. If the script is strong, you can do less than you think. Let them see for an instant what there is to be afraid of, and then let it sit inside you waiting while they sweat. When the explosion comes, commit to it completely, but it is the moments before the explosion that terrify.

TECHNIQUE

Not what you do but how you do it. The important thing to remember is that technique is the delivery system for meaning. Technique without meaning is the worst kind of acting. It doesn't even have the charm of the heartfelt neophyte. If you learn how to penetrate and analyze text, you can turn your attention to this delivery system. The best way to improve technique is by watching veteran professionals work and dissecting how they produce their effects. Watch how they use their gestural vocabulary; how they use rhythm and the pause to create timing; how they set up the other actor; how they handle the blocking; how they make the important moments read; how they control the space; how they use vocal builds; how they deliver emphasis; how they handle laughs; how they employ pace; and how they deliver focus. You have to be patient with yourself. Technique is a living craft, and mastery is a lifelong process.

THE CURTAIN CALL

Taking the call demands making a key choice. Is the cast taking the call in character (not very often) or as themselves acknowledging the audience's thanks? I must admit a strong prejudice in favor of the latter, because that moment allows us to differentiate between our artifice and ourselves. The call needs a quick tempo during group calls and complete, seemingly unhurried moments in individual calls. The best manner during this moment of closure is a simple and direct one. Bows and curtsies should be physically completed before the actor starts to move away or off. Forced charm or a show of still being lost in the play's emotions are examples of bad taste. If the house has a balcony, be sure to acknowledge it. The curtain call still demands an element of choreography and control. At that moment, the clumsy and inept do not charm. The curtain call (oh, and I do so hate it when there isn't any—a vast pretension) is not simply an acceptance of praise, it is a simple and touching sense of oneness between actor and audience.

THE CENTRAL EQUATION

The mind is revealed in the words. Both are revealed in the body. All are transformed by the emotion. This forms a circle of connections so that it becomes impossible to tell where the starting point was. What we know is that the mind, the body, the words, and the emotions are always present as a single entity. Disconnect them at your peril.

MIDSTREAM

Usually onstage we see something we never see in life. Actors finish whatever they start. It's all so irretrievably tidy and responsible and unlikely. Simply on behalf of seeming a little more life-like, let's pick a half-dozen moments in the role where you don't finish what you start. Better yet, let's stop in the middle. You start looking for your car keys in your pocket, but you stop in the middle of the search and get lost in thought about . . . whatever. You go to the refrigerator for a slice of cake. You reach out and grab the handle, but you never open it because you decide to go read *War and Peace* instead. Enjoy yourself! What else can you half finish and never complete in this role? Start, stop, digress Or start, stop, start again. The idea of getting a new idea in the middle of something looks and feels spontaneous. It intrigues the audience with what you're suddenly thinking of and, lest we forget, seems a whole lot like our own lives.

IMPERSONATION

No, I'm not talking about your fabulous William Faulkner imitation that rolls people at parties in the aisle. I'm talking about basing a role on behaviors or vocal patterns you remember from your eccentric biology teacher in tenth grade. Don't knock it. Don't say it's artificial or technical or otherwise demeaning. It's a damn good idea used sparingly. For one thing, it's a reward for listening to all the acting teachers who told you to be observant. Here are some ground rules:

1. Don't pick up something the person observed does *all* the time. It will drive us crazy.
2. It's best to crib from two people simultaneously. It feels more like art than stealing.
3. Make sure it serves a purpose. "He always rubs his thumb and forefinger together *when he's thinking.*"
4. Choose for your model someone you think is ultimately charming, not irritating.
5. Whatever it is, don't do it more than two or three times in a scene.

Such stealing is honorable work. The best do it.

GET SOME FRUSTRATION INTO THE SCENE

It may sound ludicrous but honestly it's the actor's friend. There are two major ways to let it spice your acting. First, we have the frustration the character feels when she wants something very badly indeed and it is very very difficult to get. This sort of frustration very often leads the character into doing the wrong thing and thus making it even harder to achieve her goal. Wonderful! Doing the wrong thing then makes the character angry with herself and thus adds another dimension. The second category of frustration is minor but still fabulous. He wants her to marry him, and when he goes over to ask her, he notices he has pizza sauce on his shirt. This minor frustration in a major situation adds detail, dimensions, and (last but certainly not least) something to do. Experiment with both forms of frustration by adding a dollop to a scene that seems flat and no fun to play. It adds an odd sparkle.

Jon Jory

A Thing

Sometimes we move past the golden moment without even knowing it's there. The potential jewel often arrives within reach spontaneously while our mind is elsewhere. Yesterday, in a love scene, I saw one actor touch another actor on the arm. The second actor shook off the touch almost brutally, literally pushing his hand away rudely. This action provided a great opportunity for the rejected actor, but he didn't even notice. Why? The actor was looking beyond the present moment. He had an agenda not a consciousness. Perhaps he had other points he planned to make, and this explosive moment in the relationship (try slapping your husband's hand away and see if it gets remarked on!) just wasn't on the creative checklist. The actor needs a double-mind. One half has a plan, an action, and is pursuing it; the other half is open and aware to what is currently happening and realizes it must be incorporated and dealt with. Make sure you bring both minds to rehearsal. Don't walk past the golden nuggets on your way to somewhere else.

Finding The Attack In Defense

I was working on a scene last week where the husband finds a phone message his wife has scribbled with a man's name and hearts drawn under it. Fearing she's having an affair, he confronts her (she isn't). As soon as he attacked her, demanding she tell him what's going on, she chose a defensive position, seemingly flustered and trying to jolly him out of his mood. What would happen if she had attacked instead of defended? What if she let him know in no uncertain terms that he had *no* business prying into her phone calls and that his assumptions were demeaning to both of them? As soon as she attacked instead of defended, the scene seemed enriched, more complex, even more theatrical. What we need to remember is to examine the possibility of attack in what looks like a defensive situation. Is this always correct? Absolutely not. What is important is that we try the option to see what it produces. There are some actors who habitually prefer defense, and, frankly, it limits their casting. See if you can't find some attack in the scene.

93

THE TEASE

In strip clubs "the tease" is a piece of craft-oriented vocabulary. Let's change the context to the theater. When the line coming up will unravel the mystery, change the course of the story, set in motion the comedy or tragedy, use the tease. When the audience is dying to see or know, take a moment before you give it to them. Will she marry him, yes or no? Time for the tease. Did the butler do it? Time for the tease. Claudius is praying. Will Hamlet kill him? Time for the tease. Will Hedda really burn her lover's manuscript as she holds it near the flames? Tease! The key here is the audience's investment in the prior moment. Come on, be a little trashy, get them leaning forward in their seats. For some reason, we as actors routinely miss these possibilities. Perhaps it's because we spend a good deal of energy shutting the viewer out of our consciousness. Perhaps we think it's too brazen or gimmicky. Hey, maybe it's generous and theatrical. Tease me.

FIGHTING FOR CONTROL

A lot of times when you watch actors, they are either playing very in control or very out of control. What they are missing is all the shadings and possibilities of fighting for control. Keep an eye on your own life; this is something we do a lot. Your boyfriend has said something really demeaning that he meant as humorous, but you're at dinner with his parents. Ordinarily you'd let him have it, but now all you can do is seethe and try to pass off the moment lightly to his mom. Good acting moment. It's a little different than Stanislavski's idea of "keeping the lid on," because quite often we are trying not to let the others see the tumult we're feeling. Sometimes we do it by taking out these feelings on an activity—for example, we cut up the apples as if we were cutting up our boyfriend, but we try to cover it all with a smile. The character has to realize that there is something she wants that can't be achieved by setting these feelings and impulses free. Where are you fighting for control in your current play?

THE LIGHTBULB IN THE COMIC STRIP

One thing and only one thing is true: This is the only acting book you can buy that uses Popeye as an example. Now, Popeye, by himself, is loading refrigerators on a truck. It gets harder. Popeye can't understand why he's struggling. Suddenly a lightbulb appears over his head. Popeye realizes he hasn't been eating his spinach! He gets it, and hopefully you get it. Where are these moments of sudden clarity in the role? The acting value is often the *suddenness*. It's a flash of understanding that strikes home with real physical participation. How could your character have missed this before? He shakes his head, throws himself back in the chair, and then rises performing a little impromptu dance. By God, he knows what to do now! Mark the lightbulb moments; look for them and enjoy playing them. I'm not talking about making a comic book of your performance—the moment can be large or small. I just don't want you to miss the opportunity. And, lest we forget, it helps to tell the story.

TWO PATHS

Every speech your character has falls into two categories: 1. Your character knows what she wants to say and marshals her rhetorical devices and sub-clauses to support her major point, which she knew she was going to make from the very beginning. In other words, she has a point to make and she makes it. 2. Your character finds out what she means as she talks. She may start with a feeling and then suddenly and, to her, surprisingly makes a point or a connection. This character finds out where she is going while she goes. All acting is either one or the other. Look through your character's speeches and divide them into these two camps. Each results in a different kind of acting. We all use both these structures, sometimes within five minutes, but you, the actor, have to decide which is which. Usually the very structure of the line decides you. These, you say looking at the script, are all supporting evidence, and this is her point. She knew where she was going. Or the opposite. Just decide.

ONE THING AT A TIME

Mark Jenkins does an exercise he calls slow-talking. The idea is that you say the line and then let it breathe and occupy the space allowing your mind and heart to fill up the silence rather than quickly moving on, and moving on, and moving on. My version of that is taking one thing at a time. If the line is "What are you thinking? Why are you sitting there like that? Don't you understand what's going to happen?" It could be spoken in a rapid bunch with the single idea that the speaker needs advice and all three lines are a restatement of that need. Or you could let each line find its own need and weight before moving on to the next. Ask the question "What are you thinking?" and really expect an answer before moving on. "What's going to happen?" seems to be another crucial question, and the answer might change the speaker's direction or behavior. Use it. Use the moment where the answer should be and isn't. By giving these moments full weight, you may transform the final sentence.

TIK TOK

As a kid I loved the Oz books (there were at least thirty-six) and had particular affection for Tik Tok, the mechanical man. Both his brain function and movements had to be separately wound up. Nowadays he just reminds me of an acting problem. I was watching an audition yesterday and thinking how mechanical the actor's work seemed. What is mechanical acting? It's acting that has become lifeless through exact repetition: He made the gesture yesterday, now he's making it today. The energy in the mechanical performance seems to be expended in replication. The focus is not on the situation; it's on the presentation. Rhythms tend to be steady. Every line seems to have the same weight and importance. Eyes seem fixed. Gesture is sculpted. There are no real transitions from one idea to another. The body functions but seems devoid of impetus or impulse. The net effect matches the Oz character: It talks, it moves, but it's definitely not human. My dear actor friend, leave Tik Tok in Oz.

LEANING IN, LEANING OUT

Abstractly, we're always moving emotionally toward or away from the other character in the scene. We want to influence or are influenced or else we wish to avoid, to remain invulnerable. During one rehearsal, you might want to make this physical and visible (nobody need know but you). You'll actually, physically, lean in or move toward, or lean out and move away, as the psychology flows through the text. Doing this will bring the character's need to influence or avoid into your body as well as your thought process and will give you a new physical awareness of the character's moment-by-moment state. In a way, it's an actor's game of hot and cold. Although you may keep only a small percentage of these impulses in your final product, it can be very revealing. If you have no instinct to lean in or out, you will discover that the scene demands further work and thought.

ABSOLUTE VACILLATION

Yes, there are a few roles (damn few) where your character sets his course and pursues it to its conclusion like an arrow to the bulls-eye. The reason there are so few is it doesn't make for very interesting acting. My suggestion is to create a character who often questions his assumptions and goals. You don't want to play exactly the same in the second scene as you did in the first, right? Moments of self- evaluation and readjustment provide delicious acting changes that add a new layer of complexity. Where is that moment when a new thought creates a new action and a new direction? What's more fun for an actor than the moment when a certainty is smashed to smithereens? Better still is the series of moments when we pursue a goal, question it, give it up, try something else, and then, chastened, go back to our original idea. Remember *The Zoo Story* where the character says, "Sometimes we have to go a long way out of our way to come back a short distance correctly"? Well, the audience likes to watch that. Get off the superhighway and show us the twists and turns of the back roads.

IN-BALANCE / OFF-BALANCE

You feel this every day. One moment you're coping; you feel in charge of the situation; you're comfortable; you're competent. Moments later, you feel at sea; others are in control; you've lost confidence and you're distinctly *un*comfortable. You know how different it feels to operate out of either of these states. Being in-balance or off-balance provides a wonderful prism with which to view the scene. Which moments are which? In a complex role, you will be moving constantly between the two states. This is, perhaps, the time for two differently colored highlighters. Would it be valuable to look at the entire role in this way? The quicker the alteration of the states, the more complexly felt and received the inner state will be. In life, we often say, "If only I'd been better prepared," or "She caught me offguard." Too often onstage we react as if we had seen the punch coming, had time to think through a response and acted on it. Take advantage of your character's off-balance moments; they are a different and valuable acting universe.

ENTERTAINING

The very idea of getting up in front of people to tell a story is potentially terrifying. The idea that these same people would pay money to watch and listen could freeze the actor/storyteller in her tracks. Whatever the nature of the story, whether it's *Lear* or *Oklahoma!*, we have to face the fact that we are the evening's entertainment. Scary. What makes us worth the price of admission? What I have found to be the most stageworthy and theatrical weaponry in the actor's arsenal is simply concentration, belief, and thought process. Commit to those three parts of the work fully, and you are worth the price of admission. No ifs, ands, or buts. Audiences are still amazed and gratified by the actor's ability to seemingly live a life inside the narrative. All the other theatricalities—the juggling, the dancing, the tumbling, the wild gesticulation, the cocky presentation and vocal pyrotechnics—are all sideshows, but the three already mentioned are the main event. In a sense, these basics are the pyrotechnics. Strange but true.

Leaving Room For The Acting

An actor friend once told me after a couple of drinks that acting is what you're feeling about what you're saying. Now sometimes the feeling is simultaneous with the saying, and sometimes it's provoked or deepened by the saying. In the latter case, you are plain old going to leave some space in all the talking for the feeling to emerge. I remember reading that the eminent English director Peter Hall once told Albert Finney, during a production of *Hamlet*, that he needed to pull back the headlong energy to leave some room to examine the text. High-energy actors particularly need to heed this advice because they sometimes drive so hard that there is no room for the character to reflect on the proceedings. Reflection. Where are the moments when it's crucial to the character you're playing? And decision making. Surely every choice he makes can't be made on the fly? Hold your horses! Don't let the part run away with you. You're riding hell for leather right past the feeling.

More Ideas

I have often worked with a great American set designer whose models are so beautiful, so detailed, so time-consuming, and so expensive that it's almost impossible to bring oneself to say, "No, I don't think that's right." Or, if you are so brave, I can't imagine saying no to the second model as well. The very extraordinary nature of these models limits the free exchange of ideas and creativity. The actor often finds herself in an analogous situation with the director. In pursuit of a solution to a moment in rehearsal, she tries something, and it is rejected by this august personage. She tries again and is once more denied. At this point the actor is loathe to try again and dumbly waits for the director's solution. Don't. Part of the actor's warrior mentality lies in creating a third solution and a fourth. You must accept no from your editor, but you must step to the plate again and again. As they say in the self-help books on salesmanship: No is the beginning of Yes.

The One-Idea Syndrome

This is about the good idea turned into a bad idea through over-use. Ellen has discovered Armand, who she is dating, is a drug dealer. He comes to propose to her not knowing she's going to break it off. The actor playing Ellen assumes she is now physically frightened of Armand. When he enters, she moves behind the sofa. She moves away when he moves forward. She doesn't look him in the face. Her hand shakes when she holds out the wine glass. Enough already. This idea is now overpowering the scene and reducing its complexity. Usually these ideas that are taken too far are excellent responses to the circumstances, but because they are defendable and interesting to play, we extend them well past the time when they have made their point. The audience is likely to feel their overstatement as a kind of hectoring and become irritated by the repetition. Add something else. She's frightened but still attracted plus she's surprised by the proposal. Now the work seems dimensional. Always have more than one idea playing.

The Glass

Now here's an acting use for an old saw. Does the character you're playing see the glass of his life as half empty or half full? This tilt of the balance toward the negative or positive can create some interesting playing. It's intriguing to see the half-full people confront the bad news and the half empty, the good news. The point isn't simple negativity or optimism (who wants to see that character?), it's the challenges life provides to either attitude. I've seen wonderful comic turns based on a character finding a silver lining to catastrophe after catastrophe. "Well, since the car's totaled, we won't have to worry about that oil change." Knowing the basic tropism of the character can guide you toward a surprising acting approach and provide an unusual moment that might otherwise seem obvious. Read the script again to see which camp this character seems to fit in. What would happen if you played him the other way? It can get your juices flowing.

IRONY AND THE ACTOR

Probably better begin with the definition, huh? Irony is the use of words to express something different from and often opposite to their literal meaning. We immediately recognize this as an actor's tool, yes? Obviously, it's particularly useful in sophisticated contemporary comedy (and Molière!). Some actors have ironic natures and find such values in every text they work on. These actors can move on to the next tip. The rest of us have to decide if this particular character is a vehicle for the ironic view. If not, there might still be moments that employ it. On the simplest level it becomes a commentary on other characters, as in: "Oh, absolutely, he *loves* me [and it's destructive]," or "He has a sense of humor all right [and it's truly stupid]." The character may also have an ironic view of the situation she finds herself in, having accepted a weekend invitation from people she dislikes only to find them celebrating her. Read the role for ironic possibilities. The result may surprise you.

REACTING INSTEAD OF DECIDING

We've talked about "taped" lines (you've decided how to say them), but oh my, how about "taped" reactions? Sarah is told by William that her prized ferret is dead. As she did yesterday and the day before that and the day before that, she drops her venetian glass goblet, makes a horrified O of her mouth, and sits heavily on the packing box. As a matter of fact, she's done that in every rehearsal and performance for weeks. No doubt about it, that reaction is dead, mummified, technical, and contentless. Only the very, very best actors can do the same reaction over and over and keep it filled with interior life and the illusion of spontaneity. The rest of us are going to have to be brave enough to vary what we do. To break such a habitual moment, try doing less or, better still, nothing. Then, the next time through, tell yourself you have no idea what you'll do and let it simply happen. Or, do it ten different ways in rapid succession and pick one on the spur of the moment. Remember, we see you, and dead is dead.

SET GOALS FOR THE RUN-THROUGH

Having watched actors in the run-through process for forty years, I find they are vague about the specific value. Actors enjoy run-throughs—they need them certainly—but usually they have only a vague sense of "how they did." They tend to categorize these events as "good" or "bad" and speak generally, saying, "I just wasn't present" or "I felt like I was shouting too much" or "I liked the first act, but the second act sucked." I suggest that the actor make a battle plan for each run-through. Take a few minutes and decide what you're working on and what you want to accomplish in the next run. Include a target scene you feel is shaky and has a specific problem and decide how you will attack it tomorrow. This plan is ten or fifteen minutes well spent because it gives you a basis for judging the day's work. Otherwise, you have only the director's notes to provide an analysis, and she may not be focused on you or may react generally rather than specifically. Be proactive.

THE VALUE OF USING THE WRONG FORK

Manners: agreed-upon behavior to allow social interaction. So much of the acting work we do is built around manners. We take off our hat in the house without even thinking about it. Obviously, manners change from culture to culture, so the first thing is to understand what manners, mores, and social graces are operative in your play. Does your character know, have, and value the appropriate behavior? Is he aware that when bowling you don't make your approach at the same time as someone in the next lane? If he knows the rules, does he follow them or break them? Sometimes a defining moment is when the character doesn't or won't take off that hat. It can work both ways. You kiss a woman you only met five minutes ago, or you take off your shoes unasked in someone's home. The actor can build interesting, even telling, moments inside or outside the accepted norm. Which side is your character on, and why?

SMALL CHANGES

No matter how precise your performance has become through repeated rehearsals, no matter how many performances you have played, no matter how demanding the director, your work must remain a living thing, and living things change. You are going to have new ideas, instincts, and perceptions eight performances in. How do you know what change is allowable? Let's put it this way, the structure remains, the details change. Blocking is structure; it stays as it has been decided unless the director notes otherwise. Anything you do that the other actor has become dependent on for the structure of her performance stays. The text, obviously, stays as it is. Fights and big emotional moments with others onstage maintain their structure. The intent and function of the performance remains. But a line reading here, a gesture there, small touches of blocking, and the handling of props can change. These are living things proceeding from living, changeable consciousness. You need those changes to stay alive.

CHANGING THE MUSICAL NOTE

Sorry to seem so technical, but our century-long focus on the psychological, has sometimes made us aurally incompetent. Young actors in my classes often speak text on the same musical note for far too long. Tonalities are not lost on the audience. They hear the music of the text as well as its meaning. This implies that if the other actor has established and sustains loud, you can get your share of the stage with soft. A useful generality would be that you should never bring your line in on the same musical note that the person before you has closed with. Come in above or below. In any case, it helps to get out of your head and really listen to what sort of tonal and rhythmic work is going on so you can make your contribution to the jazz and not the monotony. Focusing only on psychology can cause you to forget the simple fact that you're not a solo; you're playing in an orchestra. Where's your note?

TWO THINGS

Everything about acting seems easier and more interesting when you're choosing between two possibilities. Hmmm, I could do this or this! While you're making choices as an actor, conceive an alternative you could toss into the mix. It gives both you and the character decisions to make and thus creates thought process. "Should I sit down next to her, which creates intimacy, or over here, which takes the pressure off?" "Should I cajole or demand?" Often the actor selects an idea out of the air and acts on it without realizing that idea could also generate a second choice with a very different outcome. See a possibility and ask yourself "What's the alternative?" The other value is that it heightens the sense of "the first time" and gives the work an edge. Don't be satisfied with the first idea. Use it as a crowbar to pry out another. Work with two, try both. It's almost a definition of rehearsal.

THE RED NOSE

The clown hides behind it and feels free. What should you use? Well, situation and circumstance of course. The more you know, the freer you feel. But at the very beginning when you're first on your feet, some version of the red nose can put you at ease until you know more. Find simple actions you know you can complete, such as tying your shoes or picking up crumbs off a table. Hide behind those. Choose a characteristic stance, a posture for sitting and something to nibble on that you keep about your person. Hide behind those. Now, you may dispense with these little securities later. They may eventually prove to be too obvious or too limiting, but never feel you have to apologize for using them to get through the first few days. Give yourself things to fiddle with in your pockets until more meaningful props emerge. Hide behind those. I knew one actor who said he always carried a little puzzle in his pocket. "It's so I have something to do until I know what to do." A little hiding is quite respectable.

THE WORK NEEDS . . .

PLAYING LEADS

Yes, the size of the role isn't everything . . . but it's definitely something. You need to play some big roles to build your acting muscles. The big role gives the actor an experience of concentration, energy, complexity, and responsibility nothing else can. It teaches you to pace yourself, to seek variety, to accept yourself as interesting, to build the character's arc, and to deal with an emotional range no small part, however interesting, can match. The large part develops your analytical skills and your technique and timing. It forces you to discover where the big moments are and lets you feel the weight of others depending on your charisma. If you find you are steadily being cast in small or supporting roles, you need to take matters into your own hands and ensure your development by self-producing or calling in I.O.U.'s or being the squeaky wheel so you can have this crucial experience. Otherwise, when that big opportunity falls into your lap, you'll make mistakes you didn't need to make.

GETTING READY

Read this as sentimental if you will, but I do believe that a life in the theater is a great privilege. Keep that in mind as the day's work begins and progresses. Any creative process has its irritations and any work with human beings its annoyances, but remember, having the job and doing the work is a state of grace. Be there early. Settle into the atmosphere. Find a way, be it meditation or your own form of centering, to leave your other life at the door. Be patient with others and the twists and turns of their processes, and they are more likely to be patient with yours. Remember that creative communication is far from perfect, you may have to work to understand what is being said to you, and even having understood, it may not work for you today but may fall into place tomorrow. Patience. Grace under pressure. Trust. These are transformative virtues for the actor. The negative feelings of anger, self-dislike, and cruel judgment make you forget your responsibility to a creative atmosphere. Bring your best.

WHY IS IT ALWAYS "THEATER 101"?

The title of this tip is actually a humorously exasperated quote from the wonderful Seattle actor David Pichette during rehearsal. Why indeed? Why are we always forgetting stuff we know perfectly well about acting while we rehearse? I've always believed the actor and the chess master have much in common. There are so many layers of meaning, technique, and emotion that one can never keep them all in action at the same time. We're always working on one thing and forgetting another. This tip is simply, don't be too hard on yourself. You're never going to get it all. The role is always going to be, tantalizingly, a step ahead of you, and that's why we can never use it up, and the fascination and frustration of the work forever remains. When you get down on yourself and allow the illusion that nothing's right and you'll never get it and you're making one rookie mistake after another to take hold, you roadblock your own work. Relax. It's always going to be "Theater 101." Learn whatever it is for the hundredth time and move on.

THE VETERAN RESOURCE

I recently directed a play that had two actors in their sixties and six actors thirty and under. What made my jaw drop were the social patterns in the green room. On one side of the room the two veteran actors chatted and on the other, the young Turks. This happened day after day, and I became more and more bemused. What were these young actors thinking? They seemed serious about their trade, they asked me questions in rehearsal, they wanted to learn (we were doing comedy and they seemed insecure about it), but they didn't seem to have a clue as to what these veteran actors had to offer. Acting is an oral tradition usually passed on through the medium of tales told of personal experience. The veterans know the answers to your problems, whatever they are. They have been there and done that. Engage the veteran actors! Pump them for stories, pepper them with questions, tell them your acting problems. They are the faculty of your graduate degree. Don't just sit there!

START SOMEWHERE

The rehearsal is over. You have one thought, one appraisal, one nightmare . . . you suck. Not only are you sure you suck, but you're pretty sure everyone else thinks so too. Agony and insecurity wash over you like a tidal wave. You could flee the country, commit ritual disembowelment, or go to work. For the sake of this tip, let's choose the latter. Our departure point is the simple idea that you can't fix everything. You will have to start with "something." Well, what's a big scene you hate? Turn to it. Pick a moment you're uncomfortable with and examine the circumstances that surround it. Hmmm. What is the action? What tactic might you use to accomplish it? Almost immediately an idea will strike you. Now pick a moment a few lines before or after the one you just worked on. After you've done three or four, you are likely to be teeming with ideas for the scene. Move to another scene and repeat the process. Move to a third scene. Now, that's enough for a night's work. Take those ideas into tomorrow's rehearsal. You'll feel refreshed and more confident. Light a candle; don't curse the darkness.

YOUR MORALITY AND ETHICS AREN'T NECESSARILY THE ROLE'S

I worked for many years with an actor of remarkable temperament and skills. She was fabulous with text, wonderfully spontaneous, transparent emotionally, and highly skilled technically as well as transformative from role to role. She had only one problem—she was embarrassed by any scene that demanded her sexuality be engaged. "I just find all of that in such bad taste," she would say, and frankly she wouldn't represent it. I know another actor who opposed all forms of violent behavior and would not even slap another actor onstage. Do not accept roles or plays that you object to morally or ethically. The script shouldn't have to change (and usually can't) to accommodate your code. Once you have accepted the role, you have accepted the morals and ethics of the character. This is professional life. When you sense resistance in yourself, you must break through it. You are not the playwright. And, you signed on.

109

WHY THIS SCENE?

This is for actors in training. Pick the scenes you use for class work carefully. I've had students say, "I'm always cast as the parent, never the love interest." So? Cast yourself as the love interest. Use your scene work to fill in gaps in your experience. Never played Shakespeare? Do the balcony scene. Never played low comedy? Do a dialogue scene from *A Funny Thing Happened on the Way to the Forum*. There are a few million books with scenes for young actors. Buy five or six or sit for a few hours in the bookstore. *Don't* waste your time by agreeing to do scenes you are not essentially interested in. These scenes should call to you; they should get you excited. This is one of the few areas where young actors can control their destinies. You need to do your research, find a dozen scenes and characters you would love to play, and even line up partners months before the class starts. You want to work with the best actors on roles you covet. If you aren't aggressive in this area, you have no right to complain later.

GETTING DOWN

Dear actor, it's a tough profession. Treat yourself gently. Remember . . .
1. Eat, sleep, get out into nature. Laugh.
2. No, you're not bad in the role, you just had a bad day.
3. You can do it. Never, ever say you can't.
4. Treat yourself to a nice work area, good light, good paper, your favorite pens and pencils. Why shouldn't the actor have good tools?
5. Go to rehearsal looking good and wearing clothes you like.
6. Go out of your way to make friends in the cast
7. All actors fear they will never be cast again. Of course you will. Dry periods are commonplace.
8. Really accept the compliments you get. You deserve them.
9. Enjoy your triumphs. Celebrate them. Give yourself presents.
10. Laugh at yourself. You're not a tragic figure.

STAMINA

I'm often surprised that many actors don't have the work ethic demanded by the profession. We know this work takes great energy and powerful concentration. Don't expect to be complimented for working hard; it's a given. Here are ten areas where that hard work is expected.

1. Learn the lines early—no ifs, ands, or buts.
2. Go over the blocking at home so you know it cold the day after it's been given.
3. When you get notes at the end of rehearsal, make the adjustment by the next day.
4. If you get line changes or cuts, they should be ready to go at the next rehearsal.
5. Your rehearsal energy and playing level should be as high at the end of the day as they were at the beginning.
6. You should play full out at techs unless instructed otherwise.
7. Don't wait until you're ready to play; play what you know now fully.
8. Stay at the required level, no matter how many repetitions.
9. Play or rehearse through colds, coughs, and minor illnesses without complaint or self-pity.
10. Stop whining and do it.

WHAT HAPPENED?

I'm obsessive enough to write down my rehearsal day. It may or may not be of use to you. At the end of rehearsal, I try to grab a quiet corner and do a five-minute take on the day's work. I ask myself only three specific questions. What worked? What didn't work? What did I learn? The trick, at least for me, lies in the specifics. I must not only say what worked but also what didn't work and why. I don't try to do an exhaustive job, just a few quick jottings. Under the "what I learned" category, I try to list things that I feel I can apply elsewhere in the script as well. What has proved useful about the habit is that because I write briefly, I tend to retain the ideas at least into the next day where they can serve as guidelines. At the end of each week, I reread the entries, which gives me a good sense of where I've stumbled without depressing myself. It keeps me from the dangerous, self-lacerating habit of generalizing about the work in a negative way. Don't let the rehearsal slip away.

STATES OF BEING

THEME

We've talked about theme threads, but we should talk about this crucial, central tool in the singular as well. Let's think of theme in the sense of practical advice you might give someone about life. Yes, this has a reductive quality, but when we think about the play too philosophically we often lose our way. So, what advice does this play give me about life? Perhaps in *Three Sisters* it tells me it is better simply to work and not try to understand why life is so painful and difficult. There is no answer in any case. After a piece of advice occurs to you, take this idea of a theme and apply it to the text. What moments in the play illustrate the theme? Some of the moments will then be clear to you as what happens when you *don't* follow the advice. Sometimes the theme will give you a spine to a certain scene and assist you in developing actions. The next day a different theme may occur to you that would focus scenes and moments in a different way. Fine, try that. We're not looking to be right. We're looking for things to test in rehearsal.

POTENTIAL

Whatever you are doing onstage—sitting, reminiscing, shouting, sharpening a knife or checking your jewelry—it is always preparation for what you do next. The present moment contains the potential for the next moment. Whenever you sit down, the audience understands you now have the *potential* for getting up, and the dramatic question is how, when and why. Thought about in this way, every choice becomes the springboard for the next choice. It energizes the actor to realize that you never end something—you are in the active stage of being about to do something. You have inhaled, so the dramatic interest lies in when you will exhale. Your hand is in your pocket, so the potential includes what will be in it when you take it out. One part of the thought process flows into another. And when you take the hand from the pocket, what's in it, when it happens and how it enlightens the scene are examples of the art of acting.

ACKNOWLEDGMENT

This is what you know that she knows that you know, etc. We frame our arguments and supplications in terms of what we know about the other character. Whenever we make requests of our mother, our lover or our brother, we do so knowing how much they already know about the background of that request. Knowing what they know, we frame our request with that in mind. When a married man brings up a story about his father with his wife, he recognizes that they have had many conversations about his father previously, and he knows his wife's attitudes toward his father, and all of that affects his telling of the story. In brief, you need to think what the other character already knows and feels about what you are going to say. Is this the first time Harry has heard that you strangled your dog? Did Harry like the dog or hate the dog? Now that you know that, how will it impact the way you tell it? We continually acknowledge the views of others whenever we speak. Use that.

FIGHTING SPIRIT

An actress friend of mine, Robyn Hunt, who also has a career in Japan, talks usefully about the term, "Fighting Spirit." The Japanese word *Zanshin* implies a state of relaxed mental alertness in the face of danger. How useful to the actor, who must develop a will for concentration as well as great stamina, which keeps her from ever giving up before this great thing (the performance) has been made. I have seen many actors show the white flag and cease striving because of difficulties with people, ideas, analysis or technique in rehearsal—sometimes, when they were poised on the brink of a breakthrough. The actor *must* remember that frustration is a creative state, the sand in the oyster, and if you have the fighting spirit to keep up the pressure on the problems, you will suddenly and often unexpectedly make significant advances. Think and rehearse to the bitter end, even in the face of difficult conditions, Philistines and horrible humans.

Jon Jory

EMOTIONS

Don't go chasing after them; don't try to force them; you can only create the conditions for them to appear. List and understand the circumstances. Play actions. Make sure there are obstacles. Determine what the play wishes to communicate and your character's responsibility to those themes. Personalize the situations you need to play and believe that if you have done those things, the emotions will come. If you run out of time, or the director is seriously on your case and you can't afford to lose the job, then obviously you're going to have to fake it. When that happens, I hope your technique is advanced. When faking it, underplay if possible or make sure you fully commit to the operatic emotion you're faking. The emotionally available actor won't have to fake, and the emotionally blocked actor won't last long in the profession anyway. Do your work, trust your work, concentrate, and usually the emotion will be there when you need it.

PLAYING WITH

The other actor is telling you what to do; are you tuned in to it? Be careful that you aren't simply playing what you planned instead of redefining the action in terms of what you're being given. Why doesn't the actor who is pursuing a tactic that the other actor has already countered *change* her tactic? Because, obviously, she isn't paying attention. If you are centered, clear-headed and fully in the world of the play, you will be reading the other and reacting. You know the difference between playing an agenda and taking what you know about the play and reacting inside that, freshly, to what's happening at the moment. It's scary because you can't completely plan for it. You have to trust that you're sure enough of the story, sure enough of the circumstances, sure enough of the action, that you can commit to the moment, at the moment and still move the play forward. To reach this moment of pure flight and freedom, drill the circumstances, know the point of the scene, be able to think as the character, and then let go and react.

You feel it, you follow it, then you consider it. The impulse is grounded by knowledge of the text and the character and the action the character pursues. Lots of things prevent following the impulse: stage fright, fear of criticism, fear of committing yourself, even fear of the other people in the room. The actor not brave enough to follow the impulse is seldom surprising. The impulse is the wellspring from which movement and gesture spring. To make acting from impulse, you must be sensitive to its stimulus. It demands concentration, focus and a belief in the scene. You have only a split second to go with it and, if ignored steadily, the impulse takes the lesson and is less often present. Let it into your body. Feel it. Commit to it. Move with it. The impulse precedes speech and then becomes it. Just remember, you always have more to lose by impeding the impulse than from following it. Because theatre is a group activity, we eventually have to *repeat* that which started as impulse. But that is performance—not rehearsal.

10 RULES OF CONCENTRATION

1. Play an action.
2. Raise the stakes.
3. Intensify the obstacle.
4. Know the play well enough to have a thought process.
5. Keep your mind onstage.
6. Respond to the other actor.
7. Set yourself demanding physical tasks. Have specific goals for the day's rehearsal
8. Eat well. Sleep well. Wear clothes you like.
9. Be grateful and excited that you have a play to rehearse.
10. Tell your fear of acting to get lost. Do something. Acting is doing.

Energy is the delivery system for the idea or action. Without the ideas, energy is callow. Without the energy, the ideas don't hold our attention. There are many talents who have everything they need except sufficient energy. Where are we to get it? From the action and from the stakes, yes, but also from our ego and our confidence. Energy is freed in the actor who feels he or she is attractive, must be paid attention to and is going to make their point so strongly that it must be listened to and acted upon. Once you feel you understand the scene or the section, begin to increase the energy until you can tell (or someone tells you) that you have reached the limit and are doing too much. We have mentioned the stakes but a rephrasing may help. Whatever your character wants, want it more. Now, want it more than that! The greatest sap of acting energy is simply the fear of acting. Get into the scene, find the action, pursue it ferociously and forget yourself. The energy will appear.

TABLE WORK

With some directors, it may be as brief as a single reading, sitting around the table; with others, it may be a full week of discussion before the blocking begins. Your job as an actor at the table is to pay attention to the whole story and to conceive the story's point, not to spend the time deciding how to say your lines. When you could, if asked, stand before the cast and tell the story of the play comfortably, you can switch your attention to your character's relationships. If you were not, in fact, the character but the proverbial fly on the wall, how would you describe your character's relationship with her husband? Now, how would your character represent it to her best friend? The table is the place to work on your list of given circumstances, to ask questions that occur to you about intentions and your character's function in the plot. It's a place to listen carefully to the other actors' instincts about their roles and to suss out what seems to interest the director about the play. Bring pen and paper and take notes or you'll forget.

THE FIRST READING

You got the part. You did a text analysis at home (beats, actions, arc, theme). You come to the first rehearsal. You're nervous. The company sits down at the table. You read the play. What's your job? You take in the other actors and what their first instincts are. You react spontaneously to what they give you. You play what you know at that time to sense the play under you as a rider might a horse. I do feel it's a bit of a pretension when people read in a neutral mode, saying, "Well, I don't know anything yet!" You don't? Haven't you been working on the text? Have you no intuitions? I usually feel that what's going on in that case is the fear of doing the "wrong thing," which is inimical to the creative spirit. By all means, do some acting at the reading. Make positive, warm contact with the rest of the cast. Begin to test your ideas. This is the start; start with something. Moving on from nowhere takes too much time.

THE MUDDLED MIDDLE

You have blocked the play and are in the midst of scenework. You've memorized (which you certainly should be with the blocking finished). Psychologically, it's tough because this is the time when you wish you were further ahead than you are. Relax and work *specifically*. If you haven't, break the big scene into actions and beats. Review what happens at the end of the play so you can build toward it. Listen hard for what the other person is playing so you can use it as a stimulus and an obstacle. Don't be afraid to talk to the other actors about the scenes. Press the director to give you feedback. Come into rehearsal with ideas about what you want to work on today. Spend a little time after each rehearsal reviewing what you accomplished and what new problems have arisen. Don't float and don't generalize. Go back to the theme threads and see how moments fit in. Don't keep doing the same thing when you don't know if it's the best thing.

RUN-THROUGHS

Naturally, you're happy. You've been doing piecework, and now you want to feel the fabric whole. As you begin run-throughs, what should you be working on? Pay special attention to the arc of the role to make sure you aren't playing the same thing at the beginning as you are at the end. You should be identifying beats that simply aren't playing well. Check the action; check the obstacle; check the tactics. Solving one tricky moment may suddenly clear up several others. Don't float now. Your creative powers are energized and your knowledge of the script at its height. Keep trying moments in a different way. Add a new tactic to an old action. Make sure the final scene is cumulative; that earlier scenes and attitudes and actions have set it up. We want the final moments to be a payoff, not a repetition. After the run-through, find a quiet time to not only go over the notes you've been given but to write your own notes on the run-through to form the basis for the next day's work. Try to work on small sections and avoid generalizing on the whole sweep of the role. Hopefully, the director is doing the same. This is no time to work on "everything."

OPENING NIGHT

It's here. First of all, don't get yourself jacked up. Don't run in place, inhale chocolate or do dozens of sit-ups. You want to be calm and centered. The point now is *not* to do it *even better* than you've done it before, you want to deliver it *as you rehearsed it*. You're nervous; don't make your nerves a burden for others. Rituals are fine; don't disturb others with them, and respect theirs. Be there early; avoid rushing. In the old days, most people got there an hour early. Opening night gifts and notes are optional; wishing others well sincerely and simply is standard. Designers and running crew are opening too. This is not a time to borrow other people's scripts; they may need them. Be completely ready well ahead of places. Don't suddenly bring up new ideas or solutions with your fellow actors. Don't make a show of your adrenaline rush. Don't depress everyone by saying it isn't going well. Tell yourself the story of the play so that you won't be lost in the details. Go over the given circumstances that surround your first entrance. Perform. Party.

MAINTAINING THE PERFORMANCE

You're open. While you can keep making *small* adjustments, you are responsible for maintaining the shape. Without a directorial okay, you may not change the blocking, which has become an integral part of the timing. If the director isn't available, ask the stage manager to call and ask if you may make a change. Pace is another problem, because often the actor is unaware that it has changed significantly. I have come back to see work after two weeks to find the speed has doubled or else that it has become a Swiss cheese of pauses. Be sensitive to the rhythms you opened with and fight to maintain them. The really bad news is when the actor changes the whole tone of a key scene. In a new work, I came the third night to find that a cool, ascerbic, objective marital disagreement had become a weeping, sentimental morass, replete with spontaneous kneeling! That, to the director, lets loose the dogs of war. Don't change the tone! Yes, change a line reading or two, or six, as long as the point remains the same. That doesn't mean to change two dozen. This is an eternal battle. The actor wants to grow, and the director (usually) to maintain. Unfortunately, the actor's growth is often unseemly and undisciplined. The director, being the outside eye, needs to win.

BUILDING THE ROLE

Go Out/Go In

Yes, the scene is between you and that's where you want to keep it but, in our lives, we move back and forth between our relationships with others and our relationship with ourselves. One moment we pursue an action to make the other do our will, and in the next we examine our *motives* for doing it. Narcissism is our interest in ourselves to the exclusion of the other. What the actor wants is the vacillation between the other and the self. That constant movement between, say, "Won't you please love me," and "Am I worth loving," gives your acting both a mercurial and realistic feel. The best acting is often the mind that constantly switches between these two force fields rapidly. Remember that your character has a moral and ethical sense constantly in play as self-examination and a self-critical habit of mind that keeps score even as the character relates. A character that only goes out is callow, and that only goes in is infuriating. Out and in. In and out. That's the ticket.

Touching / Not Touching

We are a fairly touchy culture, but we don't see a lot of touch onstage; why is that? Oh, yes, we see the handshake, the occasional hug, and the mechanics of the love scene, but that's about all. Both touching and not touching need to be set up. If your character touches as a matter of course, the moment when he *doesn't* touch will speak volumes. Same with the opposite. How will touch be useful to you in this role? If sometime in this play you were going to touch Actor B (your sworn enemy and competition for the Nobel Peace Prize), when would it be, and what important point would it make? Different targets have different impact. You might touch your teacher's hand, but would you ever in the normal course of events touch his face? Like everything else in theatre, the rare has the virtue of giving focus and demanding attention. Touch has a thousand taboos. Break them to make a point.

OPPOSITES

Every part should contain them. They are the perfect dimensional tool. You know the drill: If the character is kind, look for
the unkind moment. One wildly useful thing about opposites
is the need to define what you are doing, and playing so as to
find the opposite. They can be used in terms of your feelings for
other characters and result in moments like the impulsive hug in
the midst of a domestic quarrel. They can enlighten the actor's
physical world by creating the momentary stumble of the elegant
dowager. As a matter of fact, almost anything you establish for
your character—rhythm, tone, dress, ego placement, sense of
self—can allow you the opposite as an acting choice. This is
particularly valuable in your final week of rehearsal when the
role is substantially shaped, and you can, in the quiet of your
room, see in your inner eye your own performance, your own
patterns. That's when the opposite can really help you.

SENSE OF HUMOR

Does your character have a sense of humor? If so, how would
you describe it? She might have a sense of humor in a tragedy
and none at all in a comedy. If she does have one, it might not
be the same as your own. Sometimes it's wonderfully complex,
such as a character being satirized by the playwright who still has
personal humor worth discovering. Many performers show us
what's funny about the character, but that's not the same thing.
Giving the character a sense of humor helps the actor get inside
the role. It demands we penetrate our character's world view.
On further examination, can this character laugh at herself and,
if so, (returning to the text) when? As with many acting tools,
decisions in this line need to be made by pointing to specifics
in the text. If yes, Willy Loman has a sense of humor, in what
scene? On what line? No generalities.

CHARACTER

Some people believe there is no such thing as "character"; there is only the pursuit of the action. Maybe. The question that arises is, who is it that pursues the action? And more than that, what personal characteristics accompany the action? Fifteen people shoplifting a camera would each do it differently. Is the action paired with the personality and characteristics of the actor doing it? I would answer yes. This implies a degree of artifice and selectivity. Most obviously this would imply physical characteristics inferred from circumstances in the text. The actor would choose a limited number (three or four) and incorporate them in the pursuit of the action. There are also emotional characteristics implied in the narrative, and these also impact on the action. You need to lavish some thought on both so that the action can be colored by these emotional and physical maps.

WHAT SHE DOESN'T DO

Every hour of the day we are choosing not to do and say things. We don't because it would wreck our marriage, derail our job, and brutalize our dog. Sometimes our whole concentration is involved in not saying or doing something. Now that's a theatrical moment! Where in the play does your character have to bite her lip to keep a situation stable and positive? Where do you want to punch him out and hold on for dear life to the book you're reading to avoid it? There is also that fertile middle ground where you still say it, but you phrase-it-very-carefully! The effort to restrain yourself is rich theatrical territory. An impulse being damned gives us those wonderful moments where the actor turns slowly crimson before our very eyes. Can you make a list of things this character wants to say to those she relates to and doesn't? It's a blood brother to subtext.

LOSING THE ARGUMENT

There are a lot of acting egos that don't like to lose. They refuse to lose a point *about* the play; even more, they refuse to lose a point *in* the play. I think because acting can be so dangerous to our ego, we can become obsessively dominant. Over and over in our own lives we know that confused, frustrated, humiliating feeling of having to admit either we were wrong or surrender in the face of superior logic. Admitting either verbally or, even better, non-verbally, we gain a juicy acting moment. Sometimes such a moment can bond with the character's sense of humor; sometimes it gives us the chance to be fabulously defensive; sometimes we can be gracefully magnanimous. Look for the small losses (a character admitting they forgot to do an errand) as well as the large. Admit defeat well, badly, bluntly or with a sophisticated smile. Acting may be the only place where a loss is as good as a win. Enjoy it.

THE GOD OF VARIETY

If I have a central point about acting technique, it is contained in a devotion to variety. Great acting does more different things in a minute than good acting. In a sense, as soon as the audience understands what you're doing, it's time to do something else. Change the action, change the tactic, change the attitude, change the tone, change the rhythm, change something! The change itself provides focus to the moment when it occurs. The actor's inner monitoring system needs to know when any part of the process is going on too long. You need to train yourself to understand you've been shouting too long, been humble too long, been going quickly too long, or slowly too long, been romantic too long . . . you get the idea. Variety is usually the casualty of too few ideas, too little text analysis, no breakdown of beats and actions, and the obsessive dependence on our first idea. Oh, and the idea that we play a particular attitude superbly. Be various!

CLASS AND CULTURE

We like to think of America as a classless society, yet we know it isn't. Geographical, financial, racial and professional differences feed the acting process. Most valuable is the complexity of relating across class boundaries and cultures. Each corporation, for instance, has its own culture, and senior management will relate differently to middle management. Are your character relationships exclusively with others of the same class or culture? If not, how will it affect behavior in the scene? Would you touch the other person on the arm, given the difference? Given the differences, how is anger expressed? Find the differences between you and the other and then frame them as obstacles to your action in the scene. Go through the entire list of everyone your character plays with, and use class and culture to determine behavior. It's a rich tool.

AGREEMENT

It's exciting and rewarding to disagree onstage. Agreement for some reason seems less fulfilling. There is a giving over of self in agreement, so perhaps it doesn't so satisfy the ego. In any case, look for opportunities to bestow it on the other actor. It is particularly golden when you can find it in scenes where it might be considered surprising. Look for it in the midst of arguments, in confrontations with enemies, and at moments when it might not immediately be thought to be in your best interests. At those moments, it tells us things about your character we might never have suspected. When people onstage make a point you can second, show us. In life, we often trade agreement in one moment for their agreement with us at a later time. This sort of negotiation is often the subtext of the scene. By agreeing with some points of an opposing argument, we build credence for our own position. To show agreement is one of life's graces; to find agreement under pressure is an act of valor.

ATTACKING AND DEFENDING

If you have an active nature, you could probably categorize everything your character does and says under one of these headings. Naturally, before these categories work for you, you must define the action you are pursuing. That done, you can clearly see what attacking and defending are in relationship to the point. Because you already have a very particular sense of yourself when you are in one or the other of these modes, you can bring your own habits and mannerisms to either of the two. Running through the entire script and using two different color liners with this idea in mind may give you a fascinating overview of the part. You may even be surprised by your character's actions falling into one of these catchalls rather than the other. It also helps your script analysis as you think which category to consign a moment to. These two words are, of course, reductive because they omit agreement as a serious category, but it is a wonderful tool to freshen your understanding.

STAYING ONSTAGE

Someone once said that the two-character play is an utter bore because it is apparent to everyone that no matter what the characters say, no one can leave. Now this brings up one of the most useful questions in acting—why is your character staying on the stage during this scene. Why doesn't she leave? What crucial thing keeps her there? The question leads us to an important insight—just what is it that your character has to lose if they exit? Very often actors can articulate what they want to win, but it is equally revealing to understand what they cannot emotionally afford to lose. I ask actors what their character is most afraid of in this situation. Fear is a great motivator, and all characters are not the bravest of souls. You might think about what or who they are protecting by their presence. If you know why you *stay*, it will lead you to what you *do*.

THE ABSURD

Does your character have any sense of the incongruous and irrational? Do they have a hard time assigning meaning to their lives and actions? If so, you're lucky; it's probably a great part. With a sense of the absurd, you can find surprising moments. The character who laughs when we expected them to cry—the character who seems depressed by his good fortune—the character who feels that love is impossible even when it's what they always wanted. But most of all, play the character who realizes that, because nothing is possible, anything is possible. In the comic vein, it is simply your character's view of the absurdity of his or her position. It's the "How is it humanly possible that I've gotten myself into this knowing what I know." Not every character can or should have this sense of the world, but think for a moment if they are the rare (and sometimes damned) personality that is both inside and outside the situation at the same time.

METAPHOR—THE GAME

Doubtless, you played this game in high school. You ask questions of the other player (who has a third person in mind), such as: What machine is she? What breakfast cereal is she? What animal is she? What weapon is she? What pain is she?, etc. Immediately you note its applications for our work. Remove the other players, and ask yourself twenty or thirty such questions about your character. Write down both the questions and the answers because you need to have the full panoply of your intuitions to look over. Oddly enough, I find this even more useful to develop your character's view of other key characters he encounters. We don't simply behave, we behave in terms of what we take other people to be. The more complex your view of the other person, the more various your responses and actions will be. We need to be surprised by the character we are playing, and this old high school game has the potential to provide the necessary surprises.

ONE TIME ONLY

Rarity gives value. What are the things this character is only going to do *once* in this play? Maybe they'll only sit down once, or only touch another person once, or take only one long pause, or only cry once, or only shout once, or only slump once, or only pound the table once, or only smoke once, etc. Whatever this activity is that you are going to define as rare in your evening's work is going to give fabulous focus to an important moment in the text. This strategy is extremely useful. If this rare action also seems surprising in terms of what the audience has so far learned about your character, you get double value. I'll use the example of a king's throne. The king is dead, and his brother wants the kingdom. You immediately think of how psychologically revealing it will be to sit in his throne. Now, don't waste it by doing it three times so that it loses value, and carefully choose the moment you do for maximum impact in telling the story. Do the rare thing at the right moment and not too early at that!

FOLDING THE PLAY IN

You want to constantly build bridges between early and late moments in the play. Your character early on jokes about his sister's shoes, and just before the final curtain she dies and he picks a pair of shoes out of her closet and weeps. Make the connection between the two moments. His self-pity begins on page three in the incident where none of his school pals will lend him an umbrella, and pays off on page sixty-two when he feels sorrier for himself having to care for his mother than he does for the mother. Does his choice of a vacation in Act I relate to his choice of a wife in Act II? Fold the play in on itself through these kinds of connections, and it builds the energy and coherence of the performance. What are earlier examples of his possessiveness? What tiny detail on page two grows into the mighty oak of her self-destructiveness? Once the play is blocked and you have done a stagger-thru, take out your colored pencils and begin coding related moments; each one made conscious tightens and resonates your work.

LONG-TERM RELATIONSHIPS

Because long-term relationships provide (next to the complexities of family) so many dramatic possibilities, they are often the heart of the drama. How are we to bring such a relationship onto the stage? First, remember that almost anything said is part of an ongoing conversation. They have literally been talking about this for years. Not only have they said these things before, they are ninety percent sure what the reply will be. They are forever looking for a new way to say old things. This gives such conversations a particular tone full of shortcuts and loaded phrases. Sometimes it adds a subtext of irritation to simple exchanges, sometimes a line like, "Take out the garbage," brings a smile to the other's face, an affection for an old pattern in someone loved. The subtext in such scenes is deeper and richer and should be examined on a line-by-line basis. Simple information is likely to carry an emotional message. Each is wise about which tactics to use with each other to gain their ends. Remember to decide where each moment fits into the story of their lives.

THE DRAMATIC CHOICE

I listen with interest as actors, directors and designers debate the choice between doing the moment this way or that way. What will carry the day; will it be logic, intuition, status or emotion? Very often it's a mixed discussion with one side arguing cold, clear logic and the other side pleading psychology. I will suggest, however, that our basic rule of thumb should be, very simply, which of the two choices is the most dramatic, the most evocative and, of course, best tells the story. The audience pays their money for the most dramatic choice that makes sense given the circumstances, even if it bends the logic just a touch. You want to make the choice that raises the stakes. You want to make the choice that creates textually justified conflict. You want to make the choice that can set the pot to boiling. It's amazing to see actors attracted to the passive choice or the choice that turns the scene solipsistic instead of heightening the relationship. We want the juicy choice, the one with the most acting opportunities.

Time: How Long Has It Been?

As actors, we know a lot more about time than we think we do. Is the relationship a year old or five years old? Has she been waiting for him fifteen minutes or an hour? Has he been waiting for the job a day or for his whole life? How long is the clock of his patience? How close to the end of her endurance is she? What does time mean in this situation? There is a beginning, middle and end to any unit of time, and we behave differently in each. As he contemplates using that nine-milimeter pistol, is it distant from the use or right on top of it? Cruise through the text thinking about the impact of time on the relationships and behaviors you'll be working with. Which moments are time defined and time dependent? If there is an interim involved (a week since she's seen her mother), what has gone on during that time? What has been done, said and thought? The point isn't that time has passed, it's the impact of that time on the present. Short or long, it's the character's sense of it. The acting makes time visible.

Do Something Else

Early in my professional career as an actor, I was playing a role far beyond me in Shaw's *Devil's Disciple*, directed by an aging alcoholic Brit who might charitably be characterized as cranky. A moment wasn't working—we both knew it. "What should I do," I asked. "Something else," he replied. "But what," said I. He narrowed his eyes and was softly emphatic, "Something else." It was obviously all the direction I was going to get. I tried something. I looked at him. He shook his head, "Something else." It turned out to be wonderfully helpful, actually. I gave him choices until we hit on something better. I was freed of trying to follow an arcane explanation. It wasn't an intellectual problem. My acting self, moderately knowledgeable about the play and situation, simply kept coming up with new takes on the moment. Four. Five. Six. Bingo. It's a command you can give yourself. It is, frankly, a marvelous problem solver, particularly after a couple of weeks when the situations have become second nature but nagging problems remain.

136

THE POSITIVE OUTCOME

When we are lost in an emotional state, or utterly focused on some small detail in the scene, or simply enjoying the physical release of shouting, the detail often becomes the whole and our acting becomes sidetracked. Here's a good way to get back on the main road. Ask yourself what the perfect outcome would be for your character in the scene. Actually, make yourself say it. Having said it, compare it to your current action or behavior and see if it's moving you there. Yes, sometimes we are our own worst enemies, but while we are acting badly we are still (somewhere) aware of "the positive outcome" and the tension between this and what we are doing is very dramatic. A positive outcome in one scene might be marriage; in another, divorce. In one situation, it would be winning the lottery, and in another, a crust of bread. Characters not only need goals (very often short-term), they need hopes (very often long-term). Remember to provide both. When a scene is in trouble, remind yourself of what the character would consider "the positive outcome."

THE NIGHTMARE RESULT

Obviously, this pairs "the positive outcome" and is used in conjunction with it. "What," we ask of the character, "would be his nightmare version of what would happen in the scene?" We are all positioning ourselves to avoid the worst even if we have to give up cherished hopes. It opens up the role of compromise in characterization. Otherwise, every character would be going for broke. Unless the character has a sense of what the worst might be, they will behave without restraint. This is not to say that the "nightmare result" is either character's action. It may be something that both characters are cooperating to avoid, or it may be recognized by one as something that the unwitting behavior of the other may provoke. By articulating both the "positive outcome" and the "nightmare result," the character is positioned to work both defensively and aggressively in the same beat or scene. It helps the character understand on a moment-by-moment basis whether others are helping or hurting and develop actions to espouse the one or deflect the other.

IMAGE

There is the image the character wishes to present in each circumstance and the image he fears he presents. Both of these, once articulated, are of obvious use to the actor. The image s/he finds desirable will vary in relationship to each character and in each context. At the end of the scene, does the character feel they have successfully established themselves as they wished? This moment of summation (They bought it! They didn't buy it!) is a rich dramatic opportunity. There is also acting mileage to be had with the character who has doubts about her ability to pull off the desired effect or the character and whose mask unwittingly slips. Perhaps you can locate that chilling moment when your character realizes she is being seen through, which gives you the grand opportunity to answer the question: "Now what?" An evening at home identifying the various images presented and the moments of success and failure can add great savor to your work. The tension between image and reality adds a whole new dimension.

MAKING HEDDA EXIST

Is theatre just like life? Obviously not. There is no Hedda Gabler. She is words on paper, a literary construct. You are there to believe, as a child might, in that construct. You are there to tell the story of the play by delivering a series of acting details that assist the telling of that story. Like an impressionist or pointillist painting when seen from a distance, these details merge with your own humanity in a way that seems "lifelike." If you choose (intellectually or intuitively) details for your Hedda which do not assist the story and its metaphors, it will be considered second-rate work no matter how "life-like" or "theatrical" you feel it is. Audiences and critics, like crows, are often simply attracted by shiny objects, but that sort of acting does not deliver the play. Those people who believe that if you simply pursue the "action" the point will take care of itself overlook the point that they may not be pursuing the action that the telling of the story demands. There, I've said it, and I'm glad.

The Current

In the early part of the play, we are working to hold the audience's attention because the story and characters haven't gathered enough momentum. The major conflicts aren't yet defined. We're beginning to know the characters, but we're far from fascinated yet. There is, all around, the sense of *effort*, and then suddenly about twenty to thirty minutes in, the concentration seems perceptibly to deepen and we can feel the audience's involvement begin to carry us along. It is at this fulcrum that the actor's mental process is more likely to produce the riveting moment. It is now that the pause really reads and the outburst signifies. You can take a little more time now and not worry as steadily about your energy level. The current of the play—its narrative—is moving both you and the audience along. When the story takes hold, you must trust it and work only to reveal it and stay creatively inside it. You don't need to amaze with your acting; you need only to allow the text to play through you, to allow the story's complications to affect you and to let the climax open naturally like a rose.

The Five Senses

Your character has five senses just as you do. What role do they have in your performance tonight? Hamlet's way of touching and needing to be touched adds what to your Hamlet? Masha's sense of smell? Lear's eyes? Run each sense by your character and see which moments it illuminates. In odd, quiet moments of the role, your character will be wrapped up, lost in one or another of her senses. Great acting also has sensual impact on the audience. These are the areas that keep your work away from the musty smell of the purely intellectual. Which of the senses predominates in this character? Making such a choice can give your role a surprising center and an unusual physicality. I once saw Olivier kiss a lady's hand in a ball scene and, as she walked away, he fanned her perfume back to his nose. What a wonderful, unexpected detail! Alec Guinness used to record for us every iota of what he saw. Or, of course, you might deprive your character of a sense and experiment with the results.

THE TAXI'S WAITING

You know this one, right? In a nutshell, it means there is an outside reason why what you are doing must be completed with dispatch. The hardest sort of dispatch is when emotional resolution with another person has to be achieved under time pressure—and it's one of the most dramatic. The taxi is often an enormous help because it raises stakes and heightens obstacles. A person who *must* complete a complex task, but has insufficient time to do it, is an interesting person to watch. You have to search for these taxis because, with all you have to do, they are oddly easy to overlook. Remember when there is time pressure, the answer isn't simply to go faster; the answer is to redouble your efforts to solve the problem, to convince, to reassure, to make clear. It may actually mean going slower. Having to go slow when you need to go fast *is* dramatic.

STATUS

If class is a matter of money and tradition, status is a hierarchy conferred by what is valued in a given circumstance. For instance, a wealthy and powerful woman whose car has broken down will allow status to the miraculously available mechanic. When hungry, the head of Microsoft admits the dominant status of the person putting him on the restaurant waiting list. Our idiot brother is suddenly the high status individual who will lend us $50 when we need it. Status affects love, marriage, power, work, money and who gets to pick the movie. Mix status and situation and you have a fascinating prism to view the scene you're working on. Status is also chameleon and may change several times in a single scene as the circumstances change. Note your status versus the other characters you meet in the play. Are there relationships where we see the status change? Those moments when the status changes are important and interesting. Note them. Charting the winds of status for your character will make even scenes of exposition fascinating to work on.

COUNTERPOINT

In music, counterpoint is two separate musical lines—each complete in themselves—that when played at the same time create a third unity greater and more complex than the two parts. The actor could think of this in several ways. The most obvious would be the internal and external lines. For instance, the mind might be racing and under great pressure, but the physical work might be slow and deliberate thereby creating counterpoint with an interesting tension. On the other hand, the mind might be caught in the repetition of one thought, "I love him," while the physical life might have the variety of a six-course dinner. Counterpoint can also be of use to the actor in his relationship to the set. In an elegant setting, the actor indulges inelegant pursuits or vice versa. A third area of counterpoint would be in relation to another actor. Her rage is counterpointed by your calm. Your irony counterpoints his directness. You can find other uses for the idea. Just remember that the two melodies need to create a third that makes a point essential to the narrative.

Sussing The Director

Lucky you, you just got cast in a new Theresa Rebeck play (lord, she must write one a week!) at the Denver Theatre Center. First day of rehearsal. Now who and what is this director? When working with a new (to you) director, pay close attention to her work in the first week. Her working style makes clear what you need to provide. If she blocks tightly, then your focus will be on internal work that makes her blocking yours. If she's a consulter ("just move where you like"), then you need to be aware not only of your physical and behavioral instincts but how what you do juxtaposes with the other actors onstage *and* what it all looks like visually. If she focuses on the play's ideas, you need to find ways to communicate those ideas to the audience physically and textually. Each director leaves something for the actor to provide. Think of it as a doubles match with the director as a partner. Your process and your responsibilities vary given the director's strengths and proclivities. What will this director need from you? Watch closely.

Working With Directors

1. Befriend them; they're nervous.
2. They don't know everything. Don't expect them to.
3. Directors don't create on you; they create *with* you. Don't always wait for them; do something.
4. When you're not on, watch them. Sometimes you can only understand what directors want by watching them with others.
5. Good directors aren't asking you to do it now; they're asking you to work on it.
6. When you don't understand, say so (without hostility).
7. When you've been told to do one thing and want to try something else use the magic phrase "May I show you something?"
8. Really listen, it may be their subtext that's important.
9. Directors shouldn't make you feel foolish in front of your colleagues. That goes for you too.
10. Assume you're working with a good director until it's murderously clear you're not.
11. You won't know if an idea is right until you've given it your best shot. Try it twice without comment.

How To Bring Up Text With The Director

On the simplest possible level, directors can't think of everything. Good directors know this. Monomaniacs are hostile to the idea. If you have an idea about what something means that seems to differ from what he is telling you, you have options. You could:

1. Say nothing and play the meaning you've discovered.
2. Phrase it as a question: "Is it possible this could mean _____?" Directors find questions less threatening than statements.
3. If you're very comfortable and consider him your friend or if he seems wonderfully undefensive, just say, "I don't think that's it. Isn't it _____?"

If your problem isn't a difference of opinion but quite simply incomprehension, the useful phrase would be "Can you help me understand this?" In any case, watch your tone. Try not to sound defensive, angry, depressed, or arrogant. Treat the director as you would a valued fishing guide. If she finds you irritating or unpleasant, she won't help you find the fish.

THE DETAIL DEMON

There are directors who know or care as little about the actor's process as rocks or trees. They come in several flavors—these directors who make you wish you were dead. Today's flavor is the director who shuts down your creative process by micromanaging you early in the process. "No, no Arthur," says he. "Start the cross on the word *Excalibur*, sit on the word *aquamarine*, look at Amanda for two beats as soon as you sit, and then when she rises, cross your legs." Fun, huh? Dealing with such an obsessive is, of course, situational. If you know this demon, you can gently ask if he would let you explore some other possibilities. If you want to be extra careful not to offend, you can do as you're told and then slowly (not too much at once) explore. Most of the time the director won't insist on the original choice. If this methodology is really distressing you, ask for a meeting outside rehearsal and say you're enjoying the work, but you're not sure how to explore alternatives or contribute your ideas.

Jon Jory

Things You Deserve To Get From The Director

1. Respect.
2. A good atmosphere.
3. A spirit of enquiry.
4. An interest in clarity.
5. A five-minute break each hour.
6. The possibility of repetition when you need it.
7. An understanding you may not be able to do everything "right now."
8. Five minutes of her time some time soon.
9. An answer to the question you asked yesterday.
10. A sense that you're engaged in a difficult profession.
11. The honesty to say when he doesn't know.
12. What the play's about.
13. What the scene's about.
14. An enlivening description of the situation.
15. A grasp of or at least a curiosity about the circumstances.
16. Some sense of what you're doing right as well as what you're doing wrong.

Will you get all these things? Sometimes.

What You Don't Have To Take From A Director

1. Anything you consider in the least dangerous deserves a conversation and careful rehearsal with sufficient repetition.
2. Sexual harassment. Don't put up with it. Call your agent, go see the producer. Call your union. Leave the area.
3. Demeaning comments about your acting that don't assist in making the work better. Request five minutes after rehearsal and tell him it's hurting your feelings and you don't like it.
4. Not giving your scenes sufficient rehearsal. Pleasantly ask for more.
5. Not taking care of it for you if you can't get the other actor to stop directing you.
6. Cutting your role in a serious way without consultation. Ask to discuss it. You may win or lose, but you get to talk.
7. General rudeness to you. She may not realize she's doing it. Ask for a meeting outside rehearsal.

145

TOWER OF BABEL

What's the creative language being spoken on the production? There are so many training vocabularies and methodologies and highly personal semantics at play in the theater that the actor sometimes feels lost and confused. Is this a Stanislavski-based production? Meisner? Boleslavsky? Bogart? Suzuki? Spolin? Wilson? Brecht? The actor needs to pay special attention to the director's vocabulary during the first week of rehearsal. You may, for instance, be using the same words with different meanings. Don't be afraid to ask for clarification. Don't keep on using your vocabulary with her when it's plain she doesn't speak your lingo. If you feel simpatico with other cast members and they've worked with this director before, perhaps they can shed light over a cup of coffee. The key qualities here are trust and the desire to learn new tricks. Listen, ask, have faith. After all, what are the other options?

ASKING LATER

For the director, giving a note is a matter of timing. Will it be better heard now or tomorrow? For the actor, asking a question or giving an opinion is also a matter of timing. Very often it isn't so much about asking the director this or that, it's really a matter of getting your way, right? To accomplish this, you need to suss out the director's mood, and the mood of the rehearsal room generally. In my many years of directing, I've often been amazed by the actor's inability to recognize the wrong time to make her case. The director is harried and running late, has found out the lead needs to leave for a funeral, and just dropped his favorite coffee cup and smashed it to smithereens. The actor chooses this moment to suggest the director reblock act 2 because she's facing upstage too much. Seriously. When you have an important point to make in rehearsal, do it at a propitious moment, even if you have to wait a day or two. Sense the mood and the moment.

146

WORKING WITH THE BAD DIRECTOR

1. Disguise your opinion. Things are bad enough without her hating you.
2. Focus on the whys of the role. Usually a director would help you here, but . . .
3. Trust and follow your impulses, and don't wait to be told.
4. Think about how you fit into what the play means. Somebody has to think about the big picture.
5. Buddy up with your fellow actors so you can easily and valuably discuss the play.
6. Keep trying different things. You'll know what's best.
7. Try the horrible things he suggests, and then discard them bit by bit.
8. Say, "I might not get that right this minute," and then never get it.
9. Be polite and gracious and try to feed her ideas as if she thought of them.
10. Ask the best actor in the cast for tips.

THINGS NEVER TO SAY TO A DIRECTOR

1. Complaining about another actor. Talk about the moment not the person.
2. "I don't have any idea what I'm doing." This insults the director who is working with you on the role. Speak in specifics not in generalities.
3. Over-familiarity. Don't call him sweetie. Don't cling. Don't imply that you are great pals. Maintain a warm, friendly formality.
4. Don't say "I can't do that" until you've tried it more than once.
5. Don't say "My character wouldn't do that," or, worse, "My character wouldn't say that." It's not your character; it's the playwright's.
6. Before you disagree, ask for clarification.
7. Don't say you won't do that blocking. Do it, and then say "May I show you something else?"
8. It's dangerous to criticize the director to another actor. What if she passes it on?

9. Don't say "That isn't how I work."
10. Don't comment negatively on the production to the director. Duh.

No-No's

ANGRY TOO LONG

Actors love anger. Perhaps they haven't gotten to express enough of it personally. It seems to be an enormous amount of acting fun to rage. It feels like *ACTING*. Please remember the *action*. Angry to what end? The first burst may be impulse and, for a while, it may be carried by momentum; however, sooner rather than later, the character will have a means to an end. There will be tactics involved and those will change often. If you're trapped in loud and fast, those tactics won't read. Sustained anger needs a range of colors. Is that what you're giving? If your anger is action-based, when will you have gotten what you want or all you can? What precisely (given there is still some element of control) does this anger plan to accomplish? The very sound of anger is quickly used up onstage. You can return to that sound, but you can't sustain it too long. Look over the beats when their action changes, so does the anger.

JUDGING THE CHARACTER

In conversation or in the quiet of your room, you may make moral and ethical judgments of the character, but they must not color your text analysis or your work in the rehearsal room. If you play your judgments, you are working at a critical remove from the character, and the result is usually cold, two-dimensional and often stereotypical. Yes, there are moments when characters judge themselves, but such a moment is clearly in the text and is a function of character. Obviously, you must play from the character's point of view, not society's or the church's. Brecht and few other writers do demand that you "demonstrate" the character rather than inhabit her, but this is usually from a Marxist-Leninist perspective and extremely difficult for American actors to achieve. Play the action, not your moral or political position. A well written text will allow the audience to make such judgments based on what your character *does*. Concentrate on the doing, and all will be well.

SCENE STEALING

- Don't take focus when the moment belongs to the other actor.
- The audience will look where you look. Don't look away from where the moment belongs.
- Don't step on other's laughs (i.e., pick up the cue before the laugh can occur).
- Don't force the actor who should have the focus to play downstage.
- Don't play with props, shiny objects or fire when the focus lies elsewhere.
- Don't play front when you should focus on the other actor.
- Don't use sexuality inappropriately.
- Don't move when someone else delivers the laugh line (yes, of course, exceptions).
- Mysterious activities steal scenes. (Why is she tearing strips out of the book?)
- Don't make remarkable entrances in functional parts. Wild laughing and extended crying? Uh-uh.
- Scene stealing by definition is anything that attracts attention to an actor in a way that does not assist in telling the play's story.

BAD-MOUTHING

Here, we can be brief. If you bad-mouth other actors, the director, or anyone else on the production, they will hear about it. Trust me, they will. Someone for some reason of their own will pass it along and you'll be busted. Atmosphere and morale will suffer, and you will make enemies who somewhere down the line will retaliate. When you don't like someone else's work, suffer in silence. Eventually, you'll be glad you did.

Rehearsal Manners

- Be at the rehearsal five minutes ahead of time.
- Rehearsal is a creative gift; dress to celebrate it or at least to recognize it as an act of sharing.
- Be among the first to learn your lines. It's nice to share food.
- Don't walk in front of the director or actors while they are working.
- Don't read a book or magazine or pay bills where those working can see you. It implies they are boring.
- Don't bring the irritations of your outside life into the process.
- Have a pencil and pen and one to lend.
- If you're not the director, don't direct unless it's absolutely clear that it's meant to be a shared process.
- Say hello and goodbye to each person in the room. No one should be beneath your notice.
- Take the notes you are given; don't explain why you didn't do them previously.
- This is a group activity; don't take up more than your share of the director's time.
- A five-minute break is a *five*-minute break.
- Questions are better than statements.

The Dressing Room

Preparing for the play by dressing and making up is just that, preparation. Respect it. You are living at close quarters with other people who are getting ready to do a difficult thing and, in that situation, atmosphere is everything. That atmosphere should be friendly, civil, respectful and orderly. Nobody likes to prepare sitting next to a pigsty. Create a dressing table you wouldn't mind sitting next to. No radios, TV's or cell phones at use in the space. No competitive games (chess, etc.) unless there are only two of you. If there's food, it's nice to share. The closer to curtain, the quieter it gets. If you don't know if what you are doing is disturbing someone else, ask. It's dangerous to criticize someone not present; someone present will tell them. Hang up costumes as you take them off; otherwise, your make

153

unnecessary work for others. A good reputation enlists others to go the extra mile for you; don't let your fallen underwear undermine it. Careful of perfume and aftershave; people are allergic. No smoking. Treat your workspace with respect.

Conducting The Speech

When I wish I could tie an actor's hands down, they are usually conducting the speech. You've seen it, and unfortunately you've probably done it. There is a repetitive gesture with which the actor is pounding out the rhythm. Over and over again during a section of several speeches, this gesture repeats, making it almost impossible to understand the context in the face of the maestro conducting himself. Stop already! Yes, the speech's rhythm should infect the body of the actor, but variously, including shoulders, hips, legs and head, and not simply these endlessly chopping and flapping hands. The bad news is, you may not know when you're doing it. Ask an actor that you like, know and trust in the production if there's a section where you're using repetitive gestures. If you can't do that, sit quietly at home and run (in your mind's eye) a film of your performance. Yes, surprisingly, you have known what you're doing all along. Stop conducting.

Self-Pity

This quality should have a warning on the label: For use only with unattractive characters or for the rare comic conceit. Characters whining about their lives and conditions need to take arms against a sea of troubles and, by opposing, end them. Self-pity is not an action, it is a self-perpetuating tone. On top of everything else, self-pity doesn't produce sympathy. Sympathy and empathy are the rewards of the fighting spirit in the face of odds. Self-pity is also a passive state, rather than an active one, which is by definition undramatic. Identify the parts of the role you are playing that are likely to be infected by this scourge and pursue, in those moments, rigorous actions and tactics that this character would employ to become proactive. This probably means you should cut down on the tears, which are self-pity's handmaiden. A good available substitute for self-pity is anger. Anger at yourself for getting into this situation and anger at others for having brought you to this pass. Self-pity might be useful so that the character can recognize the danger and move on.

WASTING THE FIRST HOUR

There is a level at which we remain forever afraid of acting. This "actor fear" is the locked door which prevents our work from being as good as it should be. We think of dealing with it as "warming up," but it is a psychic state as well as a physical one. I sometimes find it amusing that I lose the first 20 minutes of rehearsal to this fear, or we can warm up for 20 minutes, which amounts to the same loss. How can we be present, warmed up and committed to an act of the imagination from the top of rehearsal? A warm-up at home? Fine. On the other hand, you can simply say to yourself that you are warmed up and ready to work! You can, as it were, throw yourself into the pool's icy water, endure the shock and come up swimming. It is an act of will in the face of fear, as well as stretching exercises. Because there is never enough time; it is crucial that you don't squander twenty-five hours of rehearsal being afraid.

THE TERMINAL CUTES

Ah yes, we all have our charms. In some of our performances, we have all too many of them. Recently I paid top ticket price to see a play where a young man came to his ex-sweetheart's apartment to make up after a large-scale relationship error. Oh, he was the very model of delicious, reticent rue. He stared at his feet, spoke sweetly and haltingly, cast his alienated partner melting glances, became tongue-tied, shuffled, and turned fetchingly pink. Who could resist him? He was a puppy in human form. I literally wanted to pet him. Then he redoubled those efforts. What began as ravishingly charming ended with my longing to drown him and the rest of his litter in a bucket of water. "Cute" in either sex can be audience-attracting but definitely in small servings and alternated with spicier fare. Don't overestimate the dose. Ask your director if you've gone over the edge. Maybe you should make this "cute" a tactic for getting a particular thing at a particular moment and not a staple of the characterization.

THE BAD ACTION

I see a simple mistake made over and over by actors when they choose an action. Don't develop an action at home that is dependent on something the other actor may or may not do. For instance, "I want her to stop crying." How do you know she'll *be* crying? Or, "I want him to stop being mean to me." Is that the only thing he can do with those lines? Whenever possible, the action you choose should not depend on the other actor's emotional state. You *can*, however, base an action on an emotional state you would like to *create* in the other, as in "I want her to finally feel free to be angry with me." Or, "I want him to express his love for me." Believe it or not, I actually heard one actor in rehearsal demand a specific emotional state from another actor! Why? He needed her in that state to play what he had decided to play. Worse, he demanded this state from an experienced actor with a notably bad temper. The rehearsal room was shortly an emotional bloodbath.

IDLING BETWEEN LINES

We've spoken about the actor whose face goes blank when it isn't his line. Watch the acting carefully in the next play you see, and you'll notice another variation of this. The actor speaking gestures heatedly while she talks. She pounds the table, she brushes back her hair, she points, she throws her hands up in mock horror. She is, all in all, a physical dynamo. Now she's not talking, she's listening, and lo and behold, she's a statue! What happened to gesture? What happened to behavior? In fact, where did her body go altogether? This actor's body is only engaged in the act of speaking, and all that means in terms of character and emphasis evaporates when she listens. Why? Does the body not engage in reaction? Do we never gesture at what we hear as well as accompanying what we say? Do we not continue to drink our milkshake while we listen? You see this odd dichotomy often in the actor who is not truly engaged in situation and circumstance. Just make sure your body stays alive more than 50 percent of the time.

EXPECTATIONS

You're a success! You did the role and everyone loved you! Enjoy it, don't try to repeat it. Take in the compliments, but don't work for the same ones next time. "You were sexy and dangerous in *Richard III*." Careful. Sexy and dangerous may be dead wrong for the next role. You could even look . . . well . . . foolish. As a young actor I had an antic physicality that girlfriends and the unknowledgeable tended to praise. Soon I was inserting lively physical eccentricities into roles as diverse as Loveborg in *Hedda Gabbler* and Thomas Mendip in *The Lady's Not for Burning*. I'd become a retrospective exhibit, and I was only in my midtwenties. How did it work? Very, very badly, thank you. And all in a misguided attempt to generate the compliments I'd gotten before. Make sure your work is devoted to revealing the text not reprising your golden oldies. You're too young to be Tony Bennett. You don't want your acting to be a badly calibrated attempt to attract a particular kind of attention you crave. Of course, you won't do that because you're smarter than I was.

ON FIRST SEEING THE SET AND COSTUMES

Costume, set, sound, light, and prop designers have feelings. You would think we wouldn't need to talk about this, but allow me to reference two recent experiences. Experience one. I went into a tech rehearsal. The first time the leading lady appeared in her third-act costume, a strapless green cocktail dress, she made her entrance, peered into the house, and quipped, "I feel like a three-hundred-pound lime." Almost everyone laughed uproariously. Guess who didn't? The dress designer. Experience number two. I was in a fitting for a play about street kids, and as one of the young actors was given his costume to put on, he said, "My God, what's this supposed to be?" Designers are creative artists working for the good of the production. Bite your tongue. Don't sacrifice your relationship with a designer to get a cheap laugh. Phrase your reactions gently, if at all. Say what parts of the costume will assist you as a character and which might be a problem and why. Diplomacy rules.

BACK-TO-BACK

Remember tone? That's when you believe "humility" or "seduction" or "bitterness" has a special sound, and you use your idea of that sound to present "bitterness." Obviously not a good idea, but there is a specially virulent form of playing tone that can truly seem foolish. Let's call it emotional illustration.

SUELLEN: I am really, really unbelievably angry with you, George. You drive me crazy.

GEORGE: Sorry.

SUELLEN: You know I love you, why on earth would you do that?

The actor, seeing the word *angry*, adopts her "angry" tone and then immediately segues to her "love" tone when she runs into that word a line later. There is no emotional segue from one feeling to the other; she simply illustrates the words with sound. It's a kind of emotional shortcut that denudes the text of coherent reality.

Oh So Sad

I recently saw a play concerning a man who comes home to discover his wife sleeping with a mutual friend. They were defensive, they hashed it out, they decided to split. Throughout, the husband and wife were deeply sad. Then they were sad some more. Finally, they *really* got sad. Dearest actor who reads these words, acting is the process of taking arms against a sea of troubles and, by opposing them, ends them. Take in the shock of the personal tragedy that afflicts and affects your character, and then soon, very soon, center your action around fighting your way out of the pit. Don't wallow! Among the awful things wallowing does to the actor is to drive him into a tone and often a passive physicality that does not move the play forward. Oh, it can be annoying! Sad is passive. Sad is self-regarding. Sad seems victimized. Sad is . . . well . . . boring. Concentrate your acting energy on what you must do, not how you feel. At the very least we want to see you fight to regain your balance. We respect the fighters.

Stage Fright

Stage fright normally occurs when you think about doing something in front of people. It usually disappears when you do it. Make sure that you see the first ten minutes of the play, or the act, as a series of simple tasks you know how to accomplish. If I tell you to go out in front of eight hundred people and tie your shoe, put the dishes away, and take out the garbage, stage fright abates. If I tell you to go out and be charming and then have a nervous breakdown, it increases. I repeat, break the first few minutes into tasks you know you can accomplish. After a few minutes onstage, it begins to feel normal, and sweaty palms dry. Drill the lines for the first ten minutes until you could say them in your sleep. Ask, in rehearsal, to make your first entrance several times. Give yourself a practical prop so you have something to do. Put things in your pockets to fiddle with. Go in with that untied shoelace and tie it. Create a beginning that feels normal and manageable. After that, you'll be fine.

Honesty And The Truth: The Fetish

OK, who can argue with honesty and truth? Every acting teacher celebrates them, parading them constantly like captives from a Roman victory. Directors speak solemnly of them as of heroes long dead. Actors pursue them without knowing quite what they're looking for. What do they mean, if anything? Usually they are a plea for the actor to remain recognizably within the parameters of circumstance, character, and plot. The danger is treating "honesty" and "truth" with the solemnity often associated with going to church. They often have the same effect on the actor as being shushed in the library. Everything suddenly gets very quiet and very small and very careful, draining the stage of sustaining energy. I'm not saying that's honesty and truth; I'm saying that's what happens when they are used as the bogeyman. My feeling is let's not talk about them any more. Let's pursue what we want from the other character within the circumstances and leave it at that.

Seven Things Directors Hate

1. They hate it when you don't write down notes at note sessions. Objectively, they want you to remember. Subjectively, they think you don't feel the notes are any good.
2. They hate it when you don't stay in the room for the complete run-through. Deep in their hearts they think you hate their work.
3. They really hate it when you sit in the tech and laugh at things that go wrong. I don't have to explain that, right?
4. They hate it when you want to have a long, serious conversation just when rehearsal has finished. Hey, they want to go home!
5. They hate it when you tell them about great productions you've seen of the play they're doing.
6. They hate it when you wear ugly, dirty clothes to rehearsal. Not only do they have to look at you all day, but they feel it's a commentary.
7. And they really, really hate it when you're late learning your lines.

160

Simply put, directors *hate it* (even if they are your pal) when you complain about another actor's work in the production. Avoid it like the plague. If a scene won't work because of the other actor, phrase the issue theoretically in terms of the other actor's character. "If my action is to get the Mayan coin, what is the obstacle?" Or, "If Jim (your character) needs to get Monica (her character) to absolve him, would Monica oppose that?" *Do not say*, "Is there anything we can do about Helen. *She's not giving me what I need.*" End of story.

MELODRAMA

The director gives the dreaded note—"too melodramatic!" The actor's usual response is to pull back the moment, do less, speak more quietly and often, that will serve the turn. It is true that unwanted melodrama is simply "too much." It is too much crying, too much shouting, too much fear, too much self-pity, and all of the above with too many gestures and too much misplaced confidence. The inappropriate chewing of the scenery reads as bad taste and embarrassing display. However, the response of getting "smaller" and doing "less" begs the point of what we should be doing. What should we do instead? You must re-study the action and obstacle. If shouting seems inappropriate and melodramatic, it is because the audience perceives it will not serve the actor to get what she wants. If the fact that the ship is sinking makes you cry, fine, but the real concentration is on getting off the ship. Melodrama usually means the actor is unsubtly trying to show what they feel instead of pursuing what they need. Yes, I know, there are melodramas, but mainly (except in *Dirty Work at the Crossroads*) we are trying to disguise the thin plot with complex, believable pursuit of actions. Yes, do less, but make sure the "less" still incorporates an action.

TONE

Tone is what you play when you don't know what you're playing. It's the idea that when you play a love scene, it has a certain "sound." There's the "angry" tone, the "charming" tone, the "shy" tone, the "humble" tone, etc. This concept of a correct tone results in a strong feeling that the scene is inauthentic, that one is being hustled, taken for a ride. Tone reduces complex interaction to a tasteless generalization. It is a clear and alarming sign that neither the actor nor the director have done their work and are involved in a transparent bluff to make up for it. The cure for tone is the action (what you want the other character to do, feel or understand). If you pursue the action, the tone will take care of itself, and because the action will change frequently, so will the tone, and thus variety is also served. The actor needs to develop an internal "tone" alert. You are, in a sense, singing the scene instead of playing it. It is demeaning to both the actor and the audience.

OVERSTEERING

There comes a time, if you are a serious, prepared actor, when you are probably micromanaging your performance. Too "heady," as they say. It has been true since the beginning *that you don't "play" your analysis.* The analysis simply provides a lake of information and a set of intellectual boundaries for the role. When you are onstage (particularly toward the end of the rehearsal period and in performance), you hope to be operating freshly and reacting spontaneously, using your "lake of information" as an impetus. The information fills your character's head in the same way your head is filled by your background and experiences. If you have thought about actions and beats and key moments and tactics and metaphor and function and subtext and arc, you are going to have to let go of your conscious mind that contains your information and *simply play it.* If you have prepared well, it will become the raw material for a spontaneous performance of remarkable clarity and complexity. Time to let go now.

PEOPLE STUFF

THE ACTOR'S GENEROSITY

Take a few minutes to go through your big scene to look for the *other actor's big moments*. It is, I think, telling that we often refer to the other actor as "my scene partner." You are, in fact, partners and you must help each other. How must you "set up" or "frame" this other actor's key moments? What do *you* need to give them to make them shine, because if you do that well you will be able to bask in the reflected light. You must raise the stakes in a way that makes what they do in response to your stimulus fascinating. Unless you *must* have your carriage *immediately* to save your brother from being eaten by wolves, the servant's line, "Your carriage waits without, Milord," won't be properly set up. Be generous to your fellow actors not only to make the play work, but also because their good opinion of you will result in other work. If you give, you will receive.

CONSULTING THE OTHER ACTORS

To get help from the other actors, you can't simply have a need, you have to have a position. In other words, they are more likely to engage with you if you can describe what you have thought the context of a moment is (even how it relates to the theme of the play) and what action and subtext you are using, and then say the moment still doesn't work and do they have any ideas. Simply put, to help you, they have to know what you've been playing and why. If no help is forthcoming, ask them to ask you some questions about the scene or moment, because these may open up areas you have never conceived. If all else fails, ask them what they would do in the moment. You don't have to take the advice, but it may provide a new path to explore. Talk about the play before you talk about a technique. Look at the big picture to help solve the small problem. Don't be afraid to open up your problem, but don't open it up to fools.

ASKING THE DIRECTOR

Preface your questions to the director with a little praise you can believe in or a little charm you don't mind lavishing. (Is this beneath you? I don't think so.) Be specific about which moments you need help with. Don't finish a run-through in the third week and then say, "I just don't know what I'm doing." That kind of generality is insulting to the director who has already helped you to shape the role. Don't come to argue, come to ask questions. Explain what you think the moment or scene is (i.e., what you've been playing), don't say you have no idea what to do. It's your job to have an idea and the director's job to help you examine it or provide new stimulus. Remember the director may be shy, too. Don't ask for an immediate answer; she may not have one. Be interested in the problem, not depressed by it. Depressed actors need therapy from the director, not problem-solving, and you're looking for the latter. The key, however, is to be as specific as possible about what the problem is.

WHAT'S A DRAMATURG?

You arrive at the first rehearsal and among the wave of introductions washing over you is one to the dramaturg. Let's go to Michael Dixon, the Literary Manager at Actors Theatre of Louisville, for a definition. A dramaturg:

- Helps find plays for a theatre.
- Helps playwrights develop their plays for production.
- Helps the director find the best production for the play.
- Helps the actor understand the background, context and meaning of the play.
- Helps the audience find meaning in its experience of the performance.

So, the person you've just met is a gold mine of information, but they are very, very busy. When you can grab the dramaturg for a moment, s/he can chat interestingly about the playwright's intent, the historical period of the play, definitions you would otherwise have to look up in the dictionary, and your character's function in the development of the theme. Dramaturgs. Well worth taking out to coffee.

Six Ways To Talk To A Dramaturg

Michael Dixon, one of the country's best, suggests:

1. You can ask for information, visual images, or research that will inspire or inform your work.
2. Do your own research as well. Be part of that conversation.
3. You could ask for video, music, take a field trip, or speak with an expert. The dramaturg can help.
4. Oh, and don't be nervous if the dramaturg takes a lot of notes during rehearsal. That's their job.
5. Don't be afraid to ask the dramaturg why a line was (or wasn't) cut from the script. Sometimes, the reasons behind such a decision can illuminate the conception or motivations of a character, his or her main action, or the style of an evolving production.
6. Naturally, different dramaturgs will see their work in various ways. Ask how they would like to be related to.

Six Ways To Talk To Your Director

1. "Hi, there are three specific moments I'd like to ask you about (four, five six)." The more specific your question, the more likely a helpful response.
2. "May I show you something?" When you have an acting idea, it's better to show than ask, but if it cuts across the director's ideas, you should ask before you show.
3. "What I'm trying to do is_____, is that what you're getting?" Very often, what you want conveyed isn't reading and you should know that.
4. "Could you say that slightly differently because I'm not 100% sure I get it?" It never hurts to be diplomatic.
5. "You gave me a note about_____; did I accomplish it?" A lot of times, you didn't.
6. "I could play this moment so that _____, or I could play it_____. Which is better?" By giving the director choices, they feel good and you have some control over the choices offered. The same thing applies to directors that applies to playwrights. Better to ask than to make statements.

Yes, yes, I know, there was this theatre you worked at where you had costumes from the first day of rehearsal, were on the set for three weeks and all the props were there a week before tech. Now forget about it; that's the only time it will ever happen. What is the rule of thumb about what you can ask for as a rehearsal aid? Ordinarily you don't get the actual furniture. Either they're still building it or they don't want you to break or soil it before tech. Very occasionally, you will get some key props (a very limited number) if they are going to be complex to handle. If you make a prop request and they say no or put you off, don't be a nuisance. Costumes doesn't like to give you the performance clothes because they are not there to see that they are properly handled and hung up. "Oh, I'll take good care of them," says the actor. But, in my experience, they never do. Shoes? Again, if they have them early (a week before tech), and you have a *special* (repeat *special*!) problem, they *may* accommodate you. The deal here is that these departments have a different schedule and different priorities. Respect them.

P.S. You can request *rehearsal* skirts and jackets (or their period equivalent).

Six Ways To Talk To A Fight Choreographer

The eminent fightmaster, Drew Fracher, says:

1. Do you want to know about existing injuries and/or physical limitations?
2. I was shown how to do that a different way; may I show you?
3. I feel safe, now how can I sell the fight and keep it safe?
4. How can I keep tabs on my speed once I get into performance?
5. Can you ask the costumer about padding (for knees, elbows, hips, etc.) for me?
6. Where can I get weaponry if I want to work out on my own?

168

Your work in stage combat always, always, always depends on the safety factors. Never, never, never try to curry favor or show your bravery by ignoring or repressing matters that concern safety. If safety is being overlooked or made fun of, it is your right and responsibility to make sure such matters are regarded seriously.

How To Handle An Interview

Jimmy Seacat, long-time regional theatre publicist, has the following tips:

- Understand why *you* have been selected for the interview so that you can provide what's needed.
- Anticipate the questions you might be asked. Think before you answer.
- Relax—be yourself. Be positive, sincere and conversational. Never bluff or be defensive.
- Be familiar with the publication, radio or television program. Get insider tips from the theatre publicist on who's conducting the interview.
- For print media interviews, assume all you say is "on the record." The interview starts as soon as you meet the journalist, and it *isn't over* until the reporter is gone.
- Dress to enhance your desired professional persona. TV is a visual medium.
- Viewer impact is based on your style, presence, voice and attitude. Oh, and mention the name of the play, the theatre and the dates—maybe even more than once.

Disputes With Other Actors

It's week two, and your Romeo, lost in appreciation of his own romantic style, does the entire balcony scene without looking at you. "Hey, lover," you fume, "is a little eye contact too hard for a Montague?" Romeo's eyes narrow, "Don't tell me how to play the part," and the squabble's on. When the going gets warm, what do you do? First of all, if a blowup starts in rehearsal, *do not* let it continue. No matter how angry you are, stop! If you indulge your irritation, you can damage the entire rehearsal period and ultimately, the production. Say, "Let's go on, we'll talk about it later." If the director intervenes and starts to deal with the problem, say, "just give me one minute." Take a step away, take deep breaths and then, diplomatically, start with the phrase, "I'm sorry." You could go on to say, "I'm overreacting, but I feel isolated in the scene and would be grateful for some help." After that, an at least civil dialogue could begin. After the theatrical disagreement has been mediated, there is more to do. You must (and it's hard) take the responsibility (I know, I know, it's not your fault) for mending the fences with your co-star. Try coffee, lunch, dinner, a small present or note. A professional must not allow a key stage relationship to remain polarized. You need a generous heart.

DEALING WITH A DIVA

You never know where power will reside in a production because the circumstances eternally change. One time, there may be an aggressive veteran actor and a passive neophyte director. The next, a guest director of reputation who rides roughshod. Another time, a neurotic producer dominates and, after that, a genuine star who dictates down to your costume. Assuming you're not the diva in question, how do you handle these situations? First, be aware of the power structure in the production. Second, use every effort not to get involved with a faction. Don't dish the participants over a beer, no matter how seductive it seems. Those who do are likely to take a fall. Concentrate on the play and the text. Defend important points that affect you, but on the basis of what's best for the text. Keep your own ego under control. Avoid matters of personality; try to stay objective. Stay away from the sardonic, the cynical and the sarcastic. If the stress and tension are overpowering, stay to yourself for the duration of the experience. Look beyond the current trouble. Gently but firmly defend the play. Above all, remain courteous and, unless in extremis, don't confront.

Simple Courtesy

You doubtless have a cell phone. The stage manager doubtless has a cell phone. Get the stage manager's number. Now, always, always, always call the stage manager if you're likely to be even five minutes late to rehearsal. Always.

How To Talk About The Scene With Another Actor

First of all, think well of him. He is your colleague, you are mutually dependent, and he might have the solution to your problem on the tip of his tongue. Then remember we are all shy and clumsy and self- centered, so be gentle and sincerely interested and at least moderately self-effacing. Now:

1. Ask questions, don't make statements.
2. Phrase the conversation from the point of view that *you* have difficulties not that *he* does.
3. Try to develop and agree on a set of circumstances that surround the scene.
4. Don't sound piqued, dominating, officious, or like a street-corner know-it-all.
5. Start by asking him to help you with something.
6. Discuss the scene as if it were interesting not frustrating.
7. Listen!
8. Get a feel for his sense of the character's relationship.
9. Move the conversation delicately toward specifics.
10. End the conversation on a good note. Smile.

Opening The Other Person Up

Ah, the gratitude you'll inspire! The director, currently thinking about his tax return, has left poor old Joey down left while you're way up by the bookcase. Not only that, but Joey is about to do his great speech about cobra venom. It's up to you to find a cogent reason (let's underline *cogent*) to move down on Joey's

171

level or below. Good actors manipulate their blocking not only to improve their own visibility but to assist in positioning others for their big moments. Remember, these adjustments must not be baldly put. The move to give another actor the dominant position still needs to be psychologically sound. Often this give-and-take of the upstage or dominant position happens several times in a single scene. Some directors are aware of having left an actor in a closed position, and others aren't. Don't feel shy about solving such a situation yourself in a blocking rehearsal. It's not unusual and will be repaid.

AND WHAT IS SHE DOING?

We are so aware, as actors, of our responsibility to *do* something that we sometimes overlook what's being done *to* us. Relax, breathe, give up your momentum for a bit, and fully take in what the other actor is doing. Now, react to what you're given. See how it forces you to adjust your action and tactics? Sometimes this "looking outward" takes an instant longer and, in fact, forces us to slow down and truly take in. Remember you are not simply "acting," you are acting in relationship to others. Remember that acting is a constant pattern of stimulus and then response. Go into today's rehearsal with a renewed resolve to hear and see through a quieted and centered spirit. Devote today to taking in; it will benefit all the tomorrows. It will refresh your work, stimulate others to make more contact with you, and deepen your involvement with the text, and by giving yourself away (so to speak), it oddly enough makes you more powerful.

HOW TO COMPLIMENT ANOTHER ACTOR BACKSTAGE

A woman you worked with in a horrible production of *As You Like It* (played in an outdoor swimming pool) has given you tickets to see her as Laura in *Glass Menagerie*. You must go. You do. She's OK. Now you have to go backstage. Here's what you do. First, simply congratulate her. What an undertaking! A difficult role and she came through. She's looking at you shrewdly: What did you *really* think? Go backstage armed with specifics. Comment really clearly on three moments you particularly liked and why. All of us hunger for this kind of attention and very, very seldom get it. Once you've done that, switch over to a couple of questions on her process. How did she work on the limp? How did she develop her relationship with Amanda? The important thing here is that we all, most of all, want the intelligent and respectful attention of our peers, and you will have done that. You didn't say it was "interesting." You didn't generalize. You praised specifics and were interested in her process. Good job.

THE OTHER GUY'S SUBTEXT

We all know subtext is a valuable tool. What, after all, are we really saying? When another actor calls our work "interesting," we may ascribe many meanings, not all of them positive. Yes, exactly! You can find whole new colors in the scene by having your character interpret the other character's subtext and respond to it. For some reason we often feel subtext is only our province. Trying to follow another's subtext deepens our concentration, changes our response and reaction, and often changes our whole take on a scene. Paying this kind of attention really makes us listen. In life, we are always interpreting what others say to us. Career diplomats read between the lines and then act on their interpretations. If we are in the least suspicious or doubtful of the other's intentions, we comb their utterances for interior meanings. Because we are trained to want something from the other actor, we should listen carefully for what isn't said to increase our chances of getting what we want. The other actor's subtext often teaches us what to play.

TYING TONE AND RHYTHM TO THE OTHER ACTOR

Not only do we need to vary tone and rhythm in our own work, we need to vary it *in relation to what the other actor is doing.* This is part of the active listening that so many trainers advocate.

Now the disclaimer on this tip is that all tone and rhythm have an internal component, but for the moment I'm going to speak technically. Your tone and rhythm (note the biblical repetition) need to take into account what the actor speaking directly before you does. Many times I see (or rather hear) a series of exchanges on one musical note that shortly makes it impossible for the audience to follow the meaning. Same with rhythm. Don't steadily pick up a rhythm from another actor. Hear what she is doing and then vary yours. Actors are far too often solipsistic on this point. Remember, the net result of a steady beat or a steady sound is likely to lull rather than engage.

DON'T PLAY WHAT THE OTHER ACTOR IS PLAYING

Unconsciously we sometimes fall in step with the other actor, particularly when he's good. I recently saw a *Glass Menagerie* where the gentleman caller seemed more sensitive and damaged than Laura and a *Look Back in Anger* where Jimmy's wife seemed angrier than he did. In comedy, I've seen an actor find a great bit of business in act 2, only to have another actor do it in act 1 in the next run-through. Sometimes it's a matter of picking up the tone, sometimes the manner, and sometimes the business. In any case, it tends to damage the point of the text or infuriate your colleagues. So much theater is dependent on opposites or differences. Romeo and Juliet are both in love, but they need differences in action and rhythm. When playing with wonderful actors, check whether you are unconsciously picking up some aspect of their performance. Bad guys aren't supposed to be just like the good guys. Celebrate your differences.

CHARACTER

SAVING SOMETHING

There is something your character never does. Whatever this is defines your character by its very absence. Now this thing that is absent will be released in your character by change or plot twist at the very end of the play. The question is, of course, what is it? Let's, for lack of a better term, call it the pivotal absence. It needs to be based deep in your character's needs and to somehow reveal the beating heart of the story being told. It might be a release of emotion dammed from the beginning of the play. It might be the smile always held back and absent until the moment of closure. It might be touching someone or something from which you have steadily kept your distance. This absence you are finally going to fill is also a metaphor for growth, decline, or important change. If you can find this sudden flowering, it can cap the role for you and the audience. What is that something in the role you're playing? What is this thing that isn't there?

CHARACTER THROUGH RELATIONSHIP

Yes, you could walk with a limp, continually eat pistachios, and develop a dynamite Missouri accent, but that's not really what character work is. Character, in the deepest sense, is explicated through relationships. How do you treat the other person? How do you expect to be treated by her? In what ways and with what limits do you express anger with this particular person? How do you curry favor with her? What is the nature of touch in this relationship? How do you dress for him? How do you set limits with him? In what ways are you prone to express weakness with him? What strengths does she assist? What does she do that drives you crazy? Make your own list. It is through these expressions of self in relationship to another that we come to know you. Work in those areas first. Then bring on the pistachios.

THE WHOLE THING

You got the role. You've read the script several times. You have the beginning of an idea about the author's intended meaning. How can you get a clear perspective on your part? Allow me to introduce you to my mother: "Well what I do, Jon, is to write out longhand every one of my lines in order without any of the other lines in between. First of all, it really helps me learn my lines, and you know I like to have them down very early in rehearsal. What I wanted to tell you, though, is that seeing my lines in that fashion really allows me to see what the part is and what it isn't. It dispels my fantasies about the part and brings home the realities. After doing this, I invariably find the part easier to understand and to act, and I stop trying to make it more than it is, which has always been my big fault. Try it with your part in *Merchant of Venice* and see if it doesn't help." (From a letter, January of 1957.)

CONFUSING FLIRTATION WITH SEXUAL TENSION

How many times, oh lord, have we had to sit through aggressive clichéd sexuality when what was wanted was simple flirting? It's a bonehead mistake and implies a lack of good sense and good taste. In addition it lacks that crucial quality, charm, and is often unlikable. It is a mistake often made by male directors working with female performers. Don't give me that look—it is. Flirtation is a sign that someone is signaling a desire for further contact and time spent with a person he is attracted to. It does not imply that sex is desired. Sexual signaling does. Are these two people ready for sex or do they want to get to know each other? Which does the text really demand? Don't mistake one for the other because the audience knows the difference and is dismayed when the choice seems mistaken or, as is usually the case, premature.

178

As we've said, you know what's coming, but your character doesn't. It's remarkable how often we are surprised in life and how seldom onstage. Allow yourself to be blindsided. What would you never have expected in a thousand years? Maybe an obstacle you hadn't seen coming bangs suddenly into you. Maybe the situation forces you to redirect your energy. Assumptions are destroyed by a piece of behavior. You're caught off balance and have to do it differently. It makes compelling moments. Remember, you're on page 65 and page 66 doesn't exist yet. Your character may project the future, but she damn well doesn't know it. Be startled, dumbfounded, caught unawares, made speechless. Respond hesitantly, even stupidly. We don't always handle surprises well. The surprises aren't always obvious; you may have to go looking for them.

WHAT YOU'RE DOING NOW ISN'T SIMPLY WHAT YOU'RE DOING NOW

A danger in the acting process is to fall into what I call "rosary acting." This means you play one "bead" at a time without relating them. At the beginning of the play, you talked about how, above all, you hate it when people are two-faced. Now, in the final thirty minutes, you're making jokes about your fiancée secretly having lunch with her old boyfriend. What might be a small moment has a different tonality because of what was earlier established. You've stated your hatred of duplicity, and now you're laughing at your girlfriend's dishonesty; you're being illogical. What if your character realized his inconsistency right in the middle of that moment? Perhaps this little thing on page 57 is part of a much larger current of the role. A small moment might reverse a large trend. The character, a drinker, refuses wine at a party. Maybe it's a sign of something larger. Ask yourself, does this line or exchange have a larger resonance? A moment might be important not for what you do, but for what you choose not to do because of earlier behaviors we've seen. What's the heredity of this moment?

SITTING, STANDING, OR LOLLING

Before you get into any big-time physical characterization—"I think he sits and cuts himself with a steak knife whenever he watches television"—let's just start with the basics. Does she have a preferred posture or position when sitting? How about standing? Weight equally distributed? Feet close together or wide apart? What's his walk? Any small nervous habits when he's bored? You'll be amazed how quickly these everyday traits add up to a highly specific character. A half dozen will be more than you need and probably more than you'll have time to absorb or allow to become second nature. The smaller these character adjustments—the less noticeable in and of themselves—the more magically transformational they make your work. "I don't know how he did it, but that's an entirely different person!" Use the small and almost invisible to layer a physical characterization—not too much or too often. And never tell what.

DOING THE WRONG THINGS

Your character isn't perfect. Sometimes she doesn't practice what she preaches. Sometimes she jumps to conclusions. Maybe patience or good taste eludes her. Possibly she unfairly takes her frustrations out on others. Could be she's a little greedy and a little self-centered. Looking for flaws in your character's character is sometimes a shortcut to getting inside the role. Some actors subconsciously need the audience's admiration and work to eliminate or play down character flaws, and what could have been a jagged study of good and evil becomes a white-wash. The interestingly flawed character intrigues the viewer and usually deepens the play (not if you're playing a six-line functional role, however). Try this: If you met your character at a party or on a long trip, how would you describe her to your delightfully cynical sister? The point, of course, is to find flaws the script really supports and that assist the telling of the tale.

Jon Jory

LOSING CONTROL

Make room for the irrational (or the apparently irrational). I was watching a *Soprano's* episode, and young Chris, Tony's nephew, was taking an acting class and doing a scene. The characters were using nonsense syllables to communicate, and after the first burst uttered by the other actor, Chris hauled off and knocked him down. Frustration apparently triggered it, and it was obviously impulsive. Impulse preceded thought or logic but in retrospect seemed completely in character, given earlier examples of Chris's hot head. Would your character ever lose control, and if so, would there be a slow build to the explosion or a trigger that releases an actor as a light switch illuminates a room? Naturally, losing control onstage is carefully contrived for everyone's safety, but if it happened in your play, where would it be and when?

THE DECATHLON

Think of the role as ten events:

1. Problem solving.
2. Working well with others.
3. Setting goals.
4. Self-knowledge.
5. Vulnerability.
6. Loving.
7. Ambitions.
8. Being centered.
9. Avoiding excess.
10. Unafraid.

Now decide which of these events your character is good at and which she sucks at. Let's say that you infer from the script that she's not very good at setting goals. Where, in what scene or scenes, is that playable in a way that illumines the text? Where is clear self-knowledge, or the lack of it, crucial to the character? What are her ambitions and how do they play out? By reading the text with this decathlon in mind, you'll begin to have a sense of the dimensions of the role. It's a way to begin.

181

KILLING LAUGHS

I know, I know, we work so hard to get our laughs, and now I'm going to talk about how to get rid of them. The unwelcome laugh at a serious moment or the small laugh that disrupts our ability to get a larger one a moment later are our targets. If the laugh falls in the middle of our line, it's our job to kill it, but if it comes at the end of our line, we must enlist the next actor who speaks to help us. Basically, you need to bury the line that provokes the laughter by coming in hard with the next line and leaving no room for the laugh. If the offending line is yours, take the emphasis off it, or create a visual or aural moment that distracts like slamming down your soft drink or looking suddenly at the door as if you'd heard something. Anything that pulls focus away from the offending moment or line will help. Sometimes you need to go to neutral because your physicality is drawing the laugh First, stop what you've been doing and then, if needs be, create a distraction. If worst comes to worst, don't let them hear the problem line.

SETUP / JOKE / REACTION

All right, this is comic structure. The setup needs to be crisp, clear and fairly loud. Depending on the circumstance, the joke itself can be thrown away or nailed. Finally, the reaction (which may get us a second laugh) needs to be visible, appropriate to the moment, and *in the clear.* The above structure will be ruined if the focus is in the wrong place. Don't be moving around (yes, anything has its exceptions) during the setup, don't be looking away (yes, anything has its exceptions) while someone else delivers the joke, and don't forget to give focus to the person doing the reaction to the joke. Elsewhere, I'll talk about holding for the laugh, but here we have to remember to respect the structure. Sometimes we're losing the laugh because the reaction to the joke isn't strong enough or visible enough. If the setup is energized, the actor can take something off the joke; if not, the actor needs to place the joke loud and clear.

HOLDING FOR THE LAUGH

The laugh hits, the talking stops. The interior and exterior life continues. At the moment when the laugh is declining and you can be heard, you pick up the next line. Simple enough. The hardest part is to find a way to continue the appropriate situational behavior so that it doesn't look like you are simply holding. If your character finds what has been said amusing, you can play that, but make sure you don't start *your* laugh until the audience starts theirs! If the point of the laugh satirizes your character, you can play that it takes a moment for your character to shake off the effects of the barb. Something physical is usually helpful so, as the laugh hits, it turns out to be the perfect time to put the book back in the bookcase. Another point: usually you don't want the laugh to go "cold" this means you slightly interrupt the end of the laugh rather than waiting for the silence. If you have started the line before the laugh, go back and repeat the line.

THE COMIC ADJUSTMENT

There is a sound and attitude in tragedy and most forms of drama that you simply don't hear and sense in comedy. It is the sound of people in situations where they may be physically or emotionally destroyed. That isn't going to happen in comedy or, if it does, no one else is going to take it too seriously. There is weeping in comedy, but it isn't catastrophic. There are heated arguments, but they aren't vicious. There are divorces but never custody battles. The problems in comedy are usually in some way remedial. The sound of comedy is the sound of actors enjoying themselves, of pleasure being taken in difficulties. In other words, we recognize from the attitude being taken to the problem that the problem will not truly draw blood. It is this sense of the actor's pleasure in the character's problems that frees us to laugh. We say about this or that person that "they are survivors," and so is your character. You can be emphatic—you can be furious—you can be frantic, but we also sense your pleasure in the state. Make sure you make this comic adjustment. Unless, of course, you don't want the laughs.

PHYSICAL COMEDY

Aside from doing a Marx Brothers musical or partnering Bill Irwin, most actors encounter physical comedy in more approachable terms. It's usually either a piece of extreme behavior under pressure (trying to hide a dead body while the police knock at the door) or a big physical reaction to surprising or enraging information (your wife tells you she's actually a space alien). This second is the land of the double or triple take, the collapse into a chair, etc. In both cases, the physical work echoes the extremity of the circumstance in the nature of the physicality. Big information or big pressure equals a *big* physical response. The actor needs to be brave, do something outsized that still suits the situation and be both fierce and fanatic in her pursuit of a solution, or wracked physically by the information. If you plan to go for it, *go for it.*

COMIC TIMING

A book in itself. The simplest way to approach it is to talk about the moments before the laugh line is delivered. The setup line comes, and then we get the chance to watch timing at work. (Get some old "I Love Lucy" tapes and sit down to be instructed.) The nature of the situation and setup usually tip the audience off that the laugh line is coming. If the payoff is obvious (your call), then you may want to jump on the "feed" and deliver the laugh immediately. If the laugh line is surprising (your call), then you may want to tease the audience by reacting silently to the feed for one to five seconds and then deliver the laugh line. If the "feed" is delivered loud and strong, you may want to almost throw away the laugh line, or if there has been a three or four line "build" to the joke, you may want to "top" the build with the joke. Sometimes you go for two laughs, with the first bring your "reaction" to the setup and the second being the laugh line. The real answer is, better than any book, study the masters.

DEADPAN

Watch Buster Keaton's silent films. His work is the definition. Comedy deadpan is simply not reacting to something anyone in their right mind would react to. A man turns and sees two hundred rhinoceros thundering into Times Square. He seems moderately interested but nothing on his face moves as he regards them. Deadpan. A man of no particular good looks stands at a bar looking over the room. A gorgeous woman dressed to kill rushes over, kisses him fervently and then rushes out the door. He never moves or changes expression. Deadpan. A man climbs Everest alone and without oxygen. He reaches the summit and finds a child running a lemonade stand. He buys a lemonade. His expression never changes. Deadpan. As in all comedy the laugh occurs because something is out of place. In these cases it's the lack of reaction. When a great reaction is demanded by the situation and noen is forthcoming we laugh. Deadpan is dependent on situation. Find the right one and use it.

THE BIG REACTION

This is literally a complete reversal of "deadpan." Here we have a giant reaction to a minimal event. Once again, dislocation is our comic hero. A man, sent by his wife, marches into a room to rid it of a mouse. He is armed to the teeth with mouse hunting gear and weaponry. The mouse enters. They regard each other. The mouse snarls. The man, fainting, falls like a giant redwood and hits the floor with a resounding crash. The audience laughs at this outsized reaction to a small stimulus. Dislocation. Laughs are surprised out of people by these dislocations. Everyone in the audience knows what size the reaction should be but that isn't the reaction they get. When you play comedy look through the script to find perfect opportunities for the deadpan or big reaction. Let's throw in the "slow burn" which is someone getting madder and madder without ever letting it out. This one demands total body reaction as the actor barely restrains going postal. His face turns red, his body shakes, his feet tap and his hands drum but by gigantic effort he doesn't give way to the anger until long after a normal person would be shouting. Dislocation. He should but he doesn't until . . . .

STRATEGY

Nudity

Some people don't mind—some do. It is the producer's or director's job to make it clear *in the audition* if any form of nudity
is demanded. If the actor won't do it, he should say so then or
inform those hiring that he would need a day or two to make a
decision. Make sure your position is clear *before* you go into
rehearsal. If, through some oversight, you find out nudity is
necessary only when you are in rehearsal, request a meeting as
soon as possible to discuss the issue. Once again, make your
position clear in terms of the specifics. Having agreed to nudity
in the role, discuss with the director how it will be handled in
rehearsal; when it will first become part of the process and who
will be in the room. Most directors will work to achieve maximum comfort for the actor in this circumstance. Some actors
will do the nudity in the rehearsal space; others prefer to wait
until the dress rehearsals in the performance space. It is better
to achieve an early agreement on who, when, where and how.
Then everyone will be prepared for the process.

Kissing

Still a potentially explosive issue, let's be blunt. No tongue, under
any conditions. If you are uncomfortable with the way you are
being kissed, go to the director and ask that it be brought up with
the other actor. If it happens again, step back and, in a calm, clear
voice, audible to those in the room, say, "Please don't do that."
With anybody but an obsessive-compulsive, that should take care
of it. If it happens in performance, go immediately to the stage
manager. If none of this does the trick, have a good, old-fashioned
fit. You don't have to put up with such behavior. You don't have
to "perform" the kiss in rehearsal until you are ready. Discuss it
with your partner. No one should be held in an embrace so strongly
that they feel trapped or claustrophobic. If it is crucial that the kiss
or embrace look forceful, the person being kissed should make it
look that way. Oh, need I say that you should go out of your way
to build a pleasant and friendly working relationship with your
partner in the love scene? Well, you should.

Rehearsal Clothes

Clothes define and stimulate the movement. For many actors, they can provide entree into the role as nothing else can. This being the case, what are you wearing today in rehearsal? If the costume will be restrictive, is it helpful to have dressed for comfort? If you'll be putting hands in pockets, do have the pockets? Clothes are behavior, and behavior is often class. If your rehearsal clothes stimulate behavior that indicates a different class than your character's, what patterning are you learning through rehearsal's repetitions? To be blunt, if you'll be wearing a jacket, wear one in rehearsal. If you don't have one, perhaps costumes can oblige from stock. Skirt length, accessories, winter overwear and shoes all have their impact. I'm not suggesting you need to rehearse in costume (though it would be nice, eh?), but you will want to rehearse the behaviors the clothes indicate or enforce. You won't be able to get it all done in tech. So what are you wearing to rehearsal today?

Danger

As in the circus where the trapeze artists check their own ropes, the actor must take responsibility for his or her safety. Others are thinking about it, but only you can care sufficiently. You're up on a stair landing and there is no safety railing? Stop and discuss it with the stage manager. You're afraid of pistols, dogs and heights? Let someone know. You see a lighting instrument wobbling, a platform separating, a co-worker drunk—call attention to it. It is your job to protect your skin. Any danger you have accepted, let's say descending a rope ladder from the grid, you should make sure it is rehearsed over and over. Even after everyone else is bored with the process, if you need another repetition, ask for it. Do not, under any circumstances, feel embarrassed in protecting yourself. Don't let jokes, sniggers, smiles, eye rolling or the irritation of others deter you from making sure the task can be completed safely.

DOING IT TWICE

"Oh, Walt," I say pleasantly, "will you get the chair from the desk as you speak, take it to the wall, step up on it and straighten the picture, and then get it back to the desk by the end of your speech." Silence. "Well," says Walt, "I won't have time." "Let's try it," I say gently. Walt does; he looks mournful. "It just doesn't feel comfortable," he intones. Now, dear reader, I will impart a simple truth that will make you beloved of the nation's directors. Don't say any of those things and, despite your doubts, just do it. Not only that, but try it at least twice (or more) before you say it won't work. You will be amazed at how your problems magically disappear after a couple of repetitions. And, because you were wise and didn't say it was impossible only to have to eat red-faced crow when it turned out to be simple the second time, you will appear to be the consummate professional. Do it twice.

SHTICK

Ah, yes, the bad old days before theory! From the early part of the century until the advent of the talkies, there were hundreds of forty-two-week stock companies hiring thousands of professional actors. That's right, forty-two plays in forty-two weeks and people did it year after year. My father and mother did seven seasons of it, and here's what went on in the green room: "Next week I'm doing the Irish accent." "You can't, I have to do it this week." "I'm using the eye patch." "I'm doing the stutter." "I've got the limp." "I've got the cigarette holder." This, my friends, was characterization, and it was taken very seriously indeed. A little cheap, a little tacky, but it was the actor's stock-in-trade. Now, we have text analysis and actions and sense memory and inner monologues (and a very good thing, too), but . . . shhh . . . come a little closer . . . don't tell anyone I said so, but maybe there's still a little room for the wonderful hokum of physical characterization and personality props. Use it carefully, and mix it with modern theory, but . . . don't tell . . . maybe it's your week for the eye patch.

191

BAD REVIEWS

It's going to happen—brace yourselves. I strongly suggest you wait at least three days before you read them at all. Most of us are too raw the day after. No matter how dismissive you are of the reviewer, they are going to hurt. Keep in mind the ordinary healing period is about a week. You won't forever feel what you're feeling fifteen minutes after you read them. As to never reading them, well, that strikes me as either too sensitive or a pretension. There are from time to time things said that you should pay attention to. As soon as you read the review, analyze to see if what it says about you is specific or general. If it merely calls you good or bad, dispose of it forever in the nearest receptacle. If it's specific, put it away for another day or two and then decide if you need to take it seriously. It's best never to talk about the reviews with another actor unless they bring it up first. Even if the reviewer is needlessly cruel and dead wrong, do not, I repeat, *do not write them a letter*. It is best to have a career unencumbered by feuds.

QUITTING AND BEING FIRED

The first time I fired an actor, we talked for three and one-half hours and nobody felt better. Brevity is good for everyone's dignity in this situation. When and if it happens (most of us have gone through it), there is little to be gained by anger, sarcasm and recrimination. Ask those doing the firing to *briefly* tell you the reasons. If they are objective, such as missing rehearsals, not learning the lines, or sucker-punching the director, and you have contrary evidence, present it (again briefly). If they still go forward, simply switch to the details of your exit (pay, transportation, housing, etc.) and leave in a calm, restrained way. If the firing is subjective, such as not "liking your work," there's no point to discussion. Leave courteously. If you handle it well, you may meet these people in changed circumstances down the road. Oh, and ask for written notice, it will affect your unemployment checks. When you quit, tell them clearly and simply why; don't be drawn into an extended conversation as your emotions may get the better of you. Say you will write a letter (if they wish) explaining in greater detail. And then don't. Simple, dignified, professional, brief.

THE BIT PART

Let's confront the facts; you *are* playing a bit part. You've tried calling it a "cameo," but it just won't wash. How can you make the most of it? Well, for one thing, be part of the cast. Just because you're playing a bit doesn't mean you are a bit. Greet people when you come into rehearsal; talk to people on the break; say goodbye to people when you leave. Be helpful when you can, and take pleasure in others' acting process. Cue people if they need it. Bring a thermos of tea with honey when someone's sick. Be courteous and committed; it will pay off both immediately and down the road. As to the role, take it seriously. I have seen actors with a dozen lines be the last to learn them. It demeans the process. Analyze what your character's *function* is. What is your part there to accomplish, in terms of the plot? If a quirk is written in, play it for all it's worth; if it isn't there, don't make one up. Give the part one characteristic, two at most. Play cleanly, simply and to the point. Figure out what the actor you're playing with needs and provide it. A good job will be noticed.

LEARNING THE LINES

My father acted in 137 films and hundreds of plays. He was a slow study and I spent a good part of my childhood cueing him. How did he doggedly learn the lines? He underlined the last five or six words of the speech that gave him the cue. He took a large index card which would obscure his own line. He would read the cue out loud (so the sound of it would get in his head) and then reply with his speech in a whispered monotone (so he wouldn't set a reading). He would go on until he forgot a phrase or line. Having forgotten, he would study the offending line, say it several times and then go back to the top of the page. He never, ever, cut himself any slack; he always went back to the top of the page. When he knew an entire page, he would go back to the beginning of the scene or act and cue himself up to the same point, where he would resume memorizing. Arduous? Indeed. But until his early 80s, I never heard him drop a single line. Once a scene was blocked, he never carried a script. "Unprofessional," he'd say.

TAKING NOTES / GIVING NOTES

First, the note on taking notes. In the notes after a run-through, have a notebook and pen. Write it down! For one thing, you will endear yourself to the director, who likes to fantasize that you're actually interested. For another, if you get more than three or four notes, you won't remember them. This is, for better or worse, one of the signs of a serious professional. Next, when given a note, don't argue, don't explain, don't make excuses, *take the note*. If you need a conversation with the director, seek her out later. It is a professional courtesy to say "thank you" as a sign that you heard and understood what was said. If you need simple clarification about the note, ask, but don't extend the conversation. As to giving notes, advice, blocking help or character tips to the other actor in the rehearsal setting, don't. Doing so is a cardinal sin. Outside rehearsal, if asked, maybe. Asking the other actor graciously phrased questions about the play over dinner, sure. Questions can open up nitty gritty issues that should be discussed. Statements, no. Build a relationship as open as possible with your co-workers. Basically, wait till asked.

THE VOCAL TOP OF THE SCENE

I've mentioned elsewhere that too much shouting is a big theatrical liability. My father used to say that you never let yourself be as loud as you could be; you always hold something back. It's all relative as well, and it brings up the point of where the vocal top of the scene or the play *is*. When directing, I'll sometimes identify it for the actor, saying this moment is probably as big as it ever gets. Like any other element in acting, you want to save something for the most important moments. *It's all about text*. If you're performing a role in a play filled with arguments, you have to work backwards (or forwards) from the wildest one. Obviously, you don't want to be shouting your way through the little argument and then just repeat it for the big one. I recently saw a production in which the work was so consistently loud that I was not only aurally repelled but had no idea which moments were important to the actor. When everything's important, nothing is.

FUNCTION—THE SECONDARY CHARACTER

All right, you're not playing the lead, you only have two scenes; what's your *job* in this play? You're not in there to demonstrate "what a piece of work is man," you're there to move the story forward by behaving in certain ways. You're there to drive the central character into a rage which makes his wife leave him so that he can move to Montana where he wins the lottery. If you don't drive him into a rage, your character is useless. What *won't* happen correctly in the play if something about your character doesn't provoke it or, at the very least, allow it to happen? Make a list. What happens *because* of your character that makes the play what it is? Once you clearly understand your function as it relates to the major characters and the play's themes, you can work backward from that understanding to develop a background and characteristics (not too many!) that lead this guy to *fulfill his function*. Anything short of fulfilling these conditions means you aren't doing your job.

WRITE THE BLOCKING

Make friends with the stage managers; they can provide you with crucial assistance. First of all, they can get you extra work on scenes where you need it. They can get you extra time for a quick change. In performance, they can mediate a dispute with another actor. They can get you more light. They can get you rehearsal props and clothes. They can calm the director if she's annoyed with you. Now, how to make friends with this paragon? Know his or her name. Bring small presents. Say hello and goodbye. Recognize their work and be interested in how they do it. Most of all, write down the blocking as it's given, even if it takes an extra minute. To the stage manager, this is an act of necessary professionalism and it saves them time and sometimes embarrassment. If no one else is doing it, so much the better. Also, learn the lines early. These two things will make the stage manager your ally, and that is no small thing.

THE TOOTHPICK

Physical self-consciousness bedevils all actors at some point,
and less experienced actors a good deal of the time. "There are no
props in sight. I'm not sitting. I'm still confused about the scene.
What (shhhh!) do I do with my hands?" I'll tell you—bring a
toothpick on with you. Immediately and amazingly, your hands
have a purpose, and that single fact sends a message up your
brain stem that all is well, and suddenly life is good again. The
toothpick is like physical therapy for the nervous system. Freed
to pay attention to the scene rather than being held in thrall to
free-floating angst, the actor begins to focus. Yes, it's a crutch
(a tiny crutch), and the time will come when you can abandon
it, but you need to be working, not worrying, and probably no
one will notice or, if they do, they won't understand its purpose.
Would a marble or a carpet tack do as well? Of course. The point
here is to solve a disabling problem immediately. Try it.

COMMON SENSE

I can't believe I'm writing this, but I've got to reaffirm your
common-sense approach to most situations and remind you to
use it while you're acting. Yesterday, I watched an actor ha-
rangue and revile his scene partner and, when asked what his
action was, he said, "To get her to say she loves me." "And in
your personal experience, have you ever," I asked, "gotten an
affectionate response when you behaved that way?" Sometimes
in pursuit of an idea or a theatrical moment, we completely forget
what we know to be true in life. The question, "Is my behavior
in this scene anything I would ever do in this situation," can
save you. If you haven't done it, or seen it, or heard of it, you
better be damn careful before you bring it onstage. People end
up using particular tactics because life has taught them they are
high percentage behaviors in terms of getting what they want.
Check your big moments—are they recognizable in the cold
light of day as commonsense behaviors?

TEXT

MINDFULNESS

There is a negative actor's mind-set that believes the audience is interested in the actor rather than the story. The actor, believing this, feels he must perform prodigiously to justify that interest. The actor justifying, pursues a course of being more energetic, more amazingly physical, funnier, wilder, faster, louder, and sexier than the audience has ever seen before. The result is usually like the seven-year-old doing anything for attention but lacks the seven-year-old's innocence and charm. The positive actor's mind-set is mindful of his role in the story, the current circumstances in which the character finds himself, the goals (actions) he must pursue to allow the story's fruition, and how to blend his acting into the chain of action/reaction. Allow the story to be the star of the endeavor. This regard for the story I would call the actor's mindfulness. It is a challenging but modest mind-set that allows us to differentiate between acting and showing off. Such a course, pursued fully, is also satisfyingly theatrical.

CLOSE ENOUGH FOR GOVERNMENT WORK

There is a class of actors who has the theatrical equivalent of perfect pitch. They innately, and usually not consciously, know how they should sound and behave in any scene. They back up this active intuition with good technique. They are confident; they move well; they can deliver on demand a close approximation of any emotion. You want angry? They got angry. You want angry with a tinge of regret and affection? No problem. The problem is there isn't any there there. It's generic, not individual. The actor is distanced from the effect she is producing at the very moment she produces it. Worse, it's addictive, and these actors can't stop doing it, because it's almost good and it's well crafted. At a casting call, where no one is perfect, they often get hired as the next best thing. Now, if you fall into this category, take the cure. The cure lies in your being willing to make yourself vulnerable onstage, vulnerable and specific. Do the following: Slow down and be truly present. Try to discover what you personally would do in the situation. Don't manufacture emotion;

break your flow, go back over the given circumstance, try to be *with* the other actor. Allow yourself not to know what you'll do next. Something genuine and surprising will happen.

CLARITY

Sometimes we don't need fabulous, explosive, wildly imaginative acting. Sometimes we don't need powerful emotion from the deepest human well. Sometimes we just need the actor to make a complicated speech or situation *clear*. I sit in theaters across the land and watch actors ladle emotion over flailing physicality, and all I can think is "*What* are they *saying*?" First, before you personalize or raise the stakes, just make sure you really know what the speech means. What's its point? How is the speech structured? Does the speaker already know the point when she starts, or does she find it as she speaks? Is the speech a carefully integrated piece of logic or a scattershot tour of her fractured emotional state? What's the relationship of the last line of the speech to the speech as a whole? If she repeats phrases, why? Is it a series of illustrations of a single point? Remember the phrase "What's your point?" Ask it of the speech, then decide how the acting builds to it.

THE HOT CENTER

In every scene there is an animating need or dilemma that underpins everything that happens. The characters don't necessarily talk about it all the time, but it remains present and not behind any digression. No matter what the actors talk about in the scene, they feel the presence of this central need and problem. In *Crimes of the Heart*, Lennie has always had a crush on Doc, but he only has eyes for her sister Meg. When he comes to tell Meg that her horse has been killed, the scene has many elements, but Lennie's attraction to him, which is never spoken of, is always present. This is the hot center of the scene, and the actors' awareness of it provides the scene's engine. Find the hot center, and then relate as many moments in the scene to it as you can. This is not only the glue that holds the scene together, but its energy source. Without it, we have only a series of moments of varying interest. With it, everything relates and gains power. Seek it. Use it.

SHAPE

Because our theater became so deeply psychological and we have balanced that with the flamingly theatrical, we tend not to study speech structure. How is this speech shaped?

1. What's it about? What is it trying to say?
2. Does it have a thesis? A moment where it declares its intent or subject?
3. Is part of the speech support material for that thesis?
4. Is there a summation where the speech's point is restated or declared?
5. What does the speech build toward? How is it structured to do that?
6. Can you outline the speech?

Once the actor penetrates and understands the structure, it often unblocks her emotionally as well as intellectually. There is usually a structure, and that makes certain demands on the actor. A little analysis will free your spontaneity.

WHAT YOU DON'T HAVE TO DO

What we all have to remember is that a well-written script makes it unnecessary to emphasize certain things. Richard III, for heaven's sake, is so evil that we don't need to play it. Romeo and Juliet are such attractive, sweet, charming, and involving roles that we needn't push those qualities. I recently directed a play in which one father's son was a school shooter and the other father's son, the victim. We inherently sympathized so keenly with these two men that the actors didn't need to play for sympathy; it was guaranteed by the text. If the actor plays what the script already provides, audience members feel that the performers don't trust them or, worse, that they are being

201

treated like kindergartners who may "miss the point." Read your script carefully so that you can see what the playwright has already done for you. Now you're free to work in the less overt areas or deliver those sides of the role that may be a tad underwritten and unspoken.

WHAT'S ALIENATION THEORY?

Let's oversimplify. It's forcing the audience to think about what's happening instead of simply being swept along by story and emotion. How does an actor do that? By adopting an ironic tone, by playing to the audience instead of to the other actor, by clarifying and teaching a point rather than embedding it in the role's psychology, by playing text and physicality as two separate tracks unrelated to each other, by adopting a mechanical physicality and tone, by playing a critique of the character rather than the character itself. It has to do with wanting the audience to think not simply feel. When does an actor employ these techniques? When study of the author's style and intent seem to demand it or when the director chooses to apply these techniques to the material. Does this imply a different relationship to character? To a degree. It assumes you want to communicate or "show" the audience members something about the character rather than allow them to take what they will. If for instance the character is seen to represent the negative characteristics of materialism, those characteristics *are* the character.

DON'T DEFANG DANGER

I was recently watching tapes of TV's *Sopranos* and became aware how dangerous most of the conversations were. Say the wrong thing and you could end up in the East River. Even ordinary conversation was a minefield. No wonder this show penetrates the national psyche. When language is potentially dangerous, it's dramatic by definition. Allow the fact of needing to tread carefully in most conversations to spice your work. Look at not only what you should say in a given scene but what you shouldn't. When is this character's dialogue treading on others' toes? The actor who hasn't spent a little time studying the needs of the other characters he interacts with often overlooks these verbal grenades. Did your character say that wittingly or unwittingly? Does calling her a "charming slut" amuse her or infuriate her? And did your character consider the difference? The language is often where the conflict lies. Don't overlook it.

THE MESSAGE

Sometimes it doesn't hurt to think a little bit about what you're delivering. What are you saying to the audience through the role? I know, I know, our concentration is basically kept on-stage, but if you are willing to admit that the playwright wants the audience to think in certain ways about certain situations, then how do you contribute to that message? Your character is, on one hand, a three-dimensional psychology with certain characteristics and, on the other, part of a metaphor or a pointed tale that instructs us how or how not to live. Your character may embody this message as a positive or a negative. If, for instance, *Romeo and Juliet* teaches us about the centrality of love, what is Tybalt's point? Tybalt prefers honor to love and is willing to die for family or nation but not romance. All I'm saying here is that characters exist as elements of a larger story or message and that we, as actors, cannot ignore that part of our job. The message provides the limits within which we create.

THE TURN

The turn is the moment when the scene suddenly sets off in a new direction. Like a race car driver, the actor needs to see the turn and negotiate it. Let's say, for instance, a couple has been arguing about money, which brings up her father who has been giving them loans. The man says, "You're dependent on him in more ways than one. He practically dresses you for God's sake." The following conversation is no longer about money but about the larger issue of dependency. This new subject calls on different feelings and recalls different conversations they have already had. The tone changes; the tactics change. The two people relate differently to this subject than the previous one. They even play in a different rhythm. The actors need to understand there has been a turn and that something new is demanded of them. It sounds different, it feels different, it is different. If you don't make this turn, we lose touch with the narrative. Read the script again and hunt them out.

REALLY ASK THE QUESTION

Actors sometimes run question marks like rural red lights. Go through your part and underline the questions as if you really wanted and expected an answer. Questions are a natural glue that tie the characters in a scene together. Where you fail to want the answer, you fail to include the other actor. Curiosity is an attractive character trait and an acknowledgment that we are not alone. Also keep your eyes open for a question placed in the middle of your speech. That's the one that tends to get lost. The actor knows that, because of the construction of the line, the question will not be answered, but your character *does not*. You ask the question, the other character doesn't answer, and you understand something new about the situation because of her avoidance. Start by asking each question with a real sense of demand. By seemingly demanding an answer, you demand a reaction, verbal or nonverbal, and the scene deepens.

THE IMPERATIVE

The imperative is the moment when you have to know, have to have, have to prevail. These are the sentences that define your character's needs, and the needs tell us who the character is. These moments are definitely not requests. You identify them immediately through the vocabulary. These lines contain the words *I must, you must, I have to, I've got to, you can't.* They bear down on defining moments and relationships. They are the character's necessities, and you must act them as such. The vocabulary of the imperative implies and demands high stakes. These aren't things you simply want. They are things you must have. Go through the play and underline these imperatives. Very often they get overlooked when the actor has some momentum going. Sometimes it's simply a matter of emphasis.

THE MID-LINE PAUSE

I remember there was something indefinable in my father's acting that made his work unusual and individual (at least in my experience), and one night it came to me: He kept pausing to think in the middle of a sentence. In one sense it was a gimmick, a technique, but he used it well, usually placing the pause after the connective. Here's how it went: "Yes, I did tell your father that and [three- or four-beat pause] to give him credit, he took it well." "I don't give a damn what you think but [three- or four-beat pause] I still want you go to with me." He was careful always to place it at the moment when the character might need to frame the way he put something. Also he used it sparingly and was careful not to do it if it would spoil the play's rhythms or sense.

TO CONVINCE, TO DECIDE, TO UNDERSTAND

Most of our acting falls into these three categories and certainly most of our long speeches. Even knowing which of these voyages you are embarked on is a great help. If, for instance, it's a speech to convince, it usually has to knock over a couple of obstacles en route. Sometimes it has to demolish the other character's positions before pressing your own. If it's a speech to decide ("to be or not to be"), it usually runs down the virtues or failures implicit in taking this or that path. If it's a matter of understanding, it analyzes, separates, defines, and compares possible meanings. This "understanding" will probably lead to action crucial to the plot. Should you mistake one for another in the text, both the psychology and the narrative may become incomprehensible. So, before you turn the acting loose, take a long hard look at what the speech is structured to do.

WHAT'S FUNNY?

The sad truth is that we're not all natural comedians and yet the gods of casting may still occasionally slip us a comic role. What is the normally skilled actor who didn't inherit Jim Carrey's gene pool to do? Well, we might have to engage in a little analysis. (Don't tell the natural comics; they'll laugh us to scorn.) Sit down in your favorite chair with your favorite chips and consider what's funny about the role. What's funny scene by scene? Usually it's a dislocation: George is focused on ice for his drink while the world ends; Suzy is in love with George who is in love with her cat. Sometimes it's a misunderstanding: George thinks Bill (who he has found in his wife's closet) is a tax collector. Sometimes it's obsessive behavior: George spits whenever he sees the color blue. Whatever it is, you need to recognize the comic machinery, so you can focus on it and play it full out. If you're not a natural comedian, focus on situation, situation, situation. If you understand how it functions, you can get the laughs that are there.

GETTING THE ACTION INTO THE WORDS

So we know we're supposed to be playing an action (what we want the other person to do, to feel, or to understand—some people call it the objective), but the problem in a lot of acting is that it never reaches the words. The line is, "Will you calm down for a minute so that we can actually have a negotiation?" In this situation, the other person has a fixed position, and if he maintains that, you won't get something crucial for you. The action is to get the other person to give a little so everyone gets a little. The action is to secure a negotiation. Now when you say the word *negotiation*, it has to *contain* your action. You have to fill the word *negotiation* with your need and longing. We could call it a matter of emphasis, but it's far more crucial. That word is a vehicle or container for your action. If we can't see and hear it in the word, we lose track of your need. When the words and your action come together, *fill* the words; otherwise the action lies dead in the water.

206

THE GORILLA ON THE TABLE

At this moment in the scene what is really being discussed? What's really at issue? Has it changed from the moment before, or is there just a distraction, and we'll get right back to it? She called him "rootless and undependable" and wanted to know where she really stood. Now they are discussing where to go for dinner, but her unanswered question about where she stands is still the gorilla on the table, and they both know it. Usually this gorilla is either a crucial question or need that demands a response. Sometimes it's unspoken but known to both parties. This gorilla stays in the minds and hearts of everyone present until it is dealt with or a larger gorilla shows up. For instance, her need to know where she stands might be superceded by his admission that he's seriously ill. In that case, we're dealing with a new gorilla. In theater, there is almost always an important issue in play. If you don't recognize what it is, you and the text have just parted company. Remember, often you start with issue A move on to subissues B and C, and then return to A with renewed vigor. Keep track. What's the gorilla?

WHAT'S THE MOST IMPORTANT LINE IN THE SPEECH?

Here's the nitty-gritty for the actor: Some things are more important than other things, and the acting is meant to make that clear. Now, how do we go about that? Well, we look for the text's central meanings all the way down to *this* speech's central meaning—and the lines that reveal or exemplify those meanings. Well, it's our job to pop them out. That which you deem important should strike directly to the heart of the play. When that happens, the line and the play's meaning cohere to give the moment extra weight and power. An actor who makes no real distinction between the wheat and the chaff renders the text inedible. The "door" seems as important as the "croissant" and the "croissant" seems as important as the "hand grenade" with which she plans to blow up her mother. By making everything important, we suck meaning from the play. Understanding the line's relationship to the play's meaning doesn't tell you how to play, but it illuminates the target you must hit.

THE FOREST FOR THE TREES

In the midst of a dozen interesting details, problems, and obstacles, have you lost track of the scene's *function?* You're playing Juliet. It's—what else—the balcony scene. OK. First, you're worried about getting hooked up with a Montague. Second, you're worried Tybalt will come out and make fish bait of Romeo. Third, you're worried Romeo thinks you're a pushover because he overheard how much you like him. Fourth, you're worried about how your mom and dad will take all this. Fifth, you're worried the whole relationship with Romeo is going too fast. Sixth, you're worried the nurse will overhear you, and you'll be grounded for a year. Altogether, you are very, very, very worried for very good reasons that are taken directly from the script. All these worries are making you very cranky with Romeo. You have lost track of the scene's function, which is to show two young people so crazy in love they would do anything to make it work. You have to meld the irritation and your love. As you and the director chart the scene, make sure you don't drift too far from the central function. Check it.

THE ACTOR'S TIME MACHINE

Yes, there is much to be said about playing "moment by moment" and "being in the moment," but remember, time intersects. Look through the scene. Where does the present moment collide with the character's or story's past? It may be when he realizes he is treating his new love much as he treated his ex-wife. Is it when she realizes how much like her mother she is? These past/present moments usually have strong story significance, emotional content, and lovely acting possibilities. Even better is the moment where the past impacts the present and endangers or enlightens the future. When Cousins in *Major Barbara* understands how the munitions maker, Undershaft, has become a power for good, he realizes that, for Barbara to love him in the present, he must become the Undershaft of the future. It's an ecstatic, unforgettable instant of theater created by time colliding. Comb the script for such moments. They are pure acting heaven.

DESCRIBING THE INDESCRIBABLE

You come home from the concert and Uncle Andy turns to you and says, "So what was the Brahms like?" How the hell are you going to describe that music to Uncle Andy so that he gets a sense of it? In a way, that's always the position the actor (or character) finds himself in. How can I describe these feelings to her? How can I describe the love I feel? How can I describe why I have to leave? Think of saying the lines as an endless attempt to describe the indescribable. In the play none of us wants to see, no one ever has to find the right words, they just say that damn text from beginning to end, no problem. In the play I want to see, the actor carves the language out of unforgiving rock. It takes effort and skill, and even when you say it the very best you can, the character knows that it's imperfect. It just doesn't quite describe Brahms's music. In the best acting, the character knows that language is an imperfect instrument. It always falls a little bit short of what's needed.

RE-READING THE SCRIPT

You read the script when you got the role. Maybe you re-read it twice. Soon, you underlined your role and, after that, you took to reading the parts you're in. Own up. Sometimes you never read the whole text again. Big mistake. Every time you learn something about your role, it can be used as a lever to learn five other things. Re-read from start to finish at least once a week and definitely once during tech. Make a list of questions you want to ask the text so you can read purposefully. "Why doesn't he say!') he loves her until page forty-one?" "What in the script defines her relationship to her father?" "Are the seeds of his leaving Kansas visible in the first to act?" "What are the signs that he is a violent personality?" That kind of question. The more you to know about the play, the more a full reading will reward you. Do one read for each major relationship. Remember that you are doing the play—not your part.

PUNCTUATION (TEXT)

Your old sixth grade English teacher was right—pay attention
to the punctuation (if you're expert at handling text, move on
to the next page, but . . .). When you first go into rehearsal on a
complicated role, let the punctuation lead you through it. When
you come to a period, bring closure to the sentence. Take a full-
beat pause and open the next sentence with new energy. The
comma is a half-beat pause. Handle the question marks as . . . well
. . . questions. When you're dealing with a parenthetical phrase,
let's hear those parentheses. Now, in case this sounds too simple
to live, allow me to point out that clarity (provided by using the
punctuation) is an irreplaceable virtue. In addition, it will let you
hear the author's rhythm and, in wild compound sentences, tip
you off as to where to breathe (full breath on the periods; quick
breath on the commas). Making sense is not, believe me, beneath
you and, though you have been reading from text since childhood,
adrenaline, nerves, lack of concentration and laziness sometime
drive us past the periods and give us not the tiniest respite on the
commas.

LANGUAGE

We are very often so focused on our internal work as actors that
we neglect the language. When directing Shakespeare, I often
say, "Hey, this is probably your one chance to say the word
'incarnadine' in public. Enjoy it." Over and over, I remind actors to use the adjectives. "Turn left at the red house." "What
house?" "The *red* house." Remember to enjoy the sound of the
words as well as the sense of the words. Actors should love
words, love meaning, love the click of final consonants, and
all the fabulous S's in Mississippi. Using the language means
hitting the key words and investing your own life and meaning
in words that have resonance for you. The actor has only the
body, the voice, the emotions and the words. Don't neglect the
latter! "Eat the words," I'll say. "Make a lip-smacking meal of
them at the same time you make sense."

THE CHERRIES AND THE BOWL

Many, many speeches the actor will confront have a particular structure one needs to be aware of. There will be a series of examples (much as a detective finds evidence) and then a conclusion drawn from the examples that in an intellectual or emotional sense "contains" them. Example: "Sam, we don't know each other very well, and that's good. I just had an abortion and I am very, very sad and pissed off. Why I got involved with you, I cannot possibly imagine. You weren't there when they cleaned me out, and that's good. I imagine you are feeling guilty, and that's good. There is nothing, and let me emphasize that, pal, nothing more to say about this. Goodbye." The important understanding for the actor is not to get lost by overemphasizing the examples and be unable to give focus to the crucial conclusion. The entire speech leads up to ". . . nothing more to say about this." Everything else is preparation. Check your script; you'll have several of these in a well written text.

KEY WORDS

The sentence needs emphasis. Where are you going to put it? Emphasis is the final product of text analysis and internal process. Sometimes emphasis lights up a single word and sometimes a group of words. So often the speeches flow by like so much undifferentiated water over the dam. Obviously, we have to give focus to key words and phrases—particularly in big scenes and important speeches. To choose the emphasis, you have to know the circumstances, the action, the obstacle and the point of the scene. Perhaps you should do some colored marker underlining in the densest and most central speeches. I know, I know. There is the danger of seeming mechanical, but I'm speaking here about helping you to think about the emphasis. Having done the thought, the homework and, yes, the underlining, you can turn the performance back over to spontaneity, intuition and your common sense. Try it and see the effects on your own work. If the underlining hurts, back off. At the very least it reminds you to make the choices, and the choices are the art.

The Three Beats In A Transition

You remember the deal on transitions, don't you? A transition is the moment when the idea or subject changes for the actor as in, "So will you marry me? Are you all right?" That moment between the "me" and the "are" is the transition. Now that transition actually has three acting parts and they are: 1. Completion—the actor finishes one idea; 2. Reflection—the actor thinks what to say next; 3. Decision—the actor decides on a new course of action and speaks. All this could take place in a pause of some length, or it could happen in a split second. The important thing is that there is *process* in moving from one idea to the next. Too often the actor, knowing full well what the next line is, omits the steps that give a visibility to thought and turns speaking from something alive to something mechanical. Does every transition have three visible parts? God no. The big ones do. The others may be happening during the preceding line,

The Memory Speech

If you're playing a part of decent size, there's probably a juicy speech about the time your mother ate road kill or the moment your brother leapt to his death from the bell tower. At this moment, most actors get a dreamy look, turn front, and indulge themselves unmercifully. It's the "big speech." Wrong. As soon as you've identified such a walk down memory lane, remind yourself it's part of an action trying to make someone else onstage do something. It's not a memory; it's a call to action. These speeches quite often harbor the play's theme, but the speech about Bob's death is really a plea that Audrey sleep with you, or that Jack lend you his car for the night. Integrate an action in the present with the speech about the past, and you will save yourself from an embarrassing indulgence. And don't turn front.

Quick And Light

"Pick up the pace. Faster. This is comedy, not Ibsen. Drive, drive!" The pace-maddened director, eyes blazing, snaps the whip and the actor troops, vocal cords straining, getting louder and faster and more emphatic, race on. This kind of pace feels to the audience as if they were trapped inside a kettle drum during an endless riff. When you add too much volume to overdrive speed, all the paying customer can do is long for surcease. Noel Coward's acting style provides the antidote. He played quickly, often very quickly indeed, but the tone stayed conversational, the articulation carefully attended to, and emphasis there was, but lightly handled. Pace, it is important to note, should not provoke the obvious strain of vocal or physical tension. As the pace increases (particularly in comedy), keep the body free and relaxed. Definitely no shouting and speeding for more than two or three lines. Great actors always keep something in reserve, and so should you. Speed also demands the occasional silence as a palate cleanser.

Small Talk

The dialogue is, "Want a cup of coffee." "No way." "Have a cup of coffee." "I said no." Is this text about coffee? Of course not. No playwright would waste time on it unless it was really about love, revenge or breaking up. The subtext for moments such as these will often lead you straight to the heart of your role and the play. Thumb through your script for the slivers of inane conversation and, so to speak, lift up the rock and see what's under there. You are probably playing at least one such section as disposable, when it is filled with opportunity. Why is she asking, and why is he declining? What's really at stake? Don't put all the effort into your juicy monologue about the death of your grandmother. Good things come in bland packages.

Shattering The Speech

When dealing with speeches of even medium length, you need to be careful of too many interior pauses or else you lose the sense of the entire speech. It is wildly seductive to play on a moment-by-moment basis, giving a new color and thoughtful pause every seven or eight words. Think, please, of the single point the entire speech is there to make (not its byways), and try playing it in something closer to a single gulp. Yes, there may be a pause or even two in amidst the five or six sentences, but probably *not* more. You may even want to run several like-minded sentences together, barely even acknowledging the periods. The idea is to communicate the speech's center, to let all its parts converge on a single point. Ask yourself to state in a single simple sentence what the whole speech is about, then make the delivery serve that.

Breath Score

Oh, yes, the jarring sound of the actor running out of breath before the end of the line. It's not such a problem when the playwright writes short staccato lines, like David Mamet, because you breathe on the periods, and there's always another one coming along shortly. The problem lies in the long, leisurely compound-complex sentence which, if you could, you'd do on one breath (to hold the meaning together), but you can't. In Shakespeare, for example, you may literally want to plan and execute a breath score. Where you breathe in these long sentences affects both the sense and emotion of the speech. The general rule is shallow quick breaths on the commas and fuller breaths on the periods. We're trying to avoid two things: having to gulp air in places that break up the speech awkwardly, and not having sufficient air to keep important ideas together for the sake of meaning.

Nailing The Plot Point

Read the play carefully (focusing on what your character says) for lines that contain plot points. If you say, "Harry hates rudeness," and later on he kills someone for it, you need to make sure your line is crisp, energized and has focus. In great plays, many, many, many things are said in the first act that come home to roost in the second act. Do you know what they are in the text you're working on? You often have to set names, dates, places and characteristics firmly in the audience's mind. If you don't, they will miss some subtlety of the text later. Sometimes it's a state, such as loneliness or anticipation or alienation, that will turn up later as a key feeling driving the action. You are leading the audience through the story. You are in charge of fixing firmly in the viewers' mind what they need to know in order to fully appreciate the story. Don't overlook the task.

The Dictionary

There is one great acting book we should all own, and that's a good dictionary. Use the one on your cell phone (and books still exist) when your character says, "That's inconsequential," do you actually know it's meanings? Can you list them now? What's the difference between terrified and frightened? If you say the word in your text, shouldn't you know? What if another character calls you crass? If you can't define the word, how do you know if it's something you actually are and need to be playing? You will learn more about your character with this book than anything except the given circumstances. Go through the text early in your process, make a list and let the dictionary instruct you. What shade of "hate" is this? If it's "intolerable," what exactly is that? I am continually amazed at the number of words whose shades of meaning and intent I have dead wrong. Maybe you will be, too.

WORD TRAILS

One useful pursuit for the actor who is studying the role would be to read for repeated vocabulary and content. We can assume that if the character can't get certain ideas or certain words out of his head, they signal some key meaning probably relating to central ideas in the text. In the first scene of *Long Day's Journey*, there is a lot of talk about food, breakfast, and family rituals which devolves into worry about health. This has obvious resonance in this great play about family dysfunction. The important point when you find these word chains is that you need to think about them in a larger metaphoric way. This play is about food in the sense of moral and emotional sustenance. What do we need to survive? It's about health, not only physically but in the context of the productive life. Once these larger issues are identified, you can see more clearly your own function as an important cog in the watch-works of the play. What words are used more than once? And what ideas?!

RHYTHM, TEMPO, TONE, AND MEANING

These four things inform every line we speak (particularly lines of three sentences and more). Rhythm is the beat, which is demonstrated for you in any jazz composition, and it constantly changes. The steady rhythm loses interest. Tempo informs rhythm with slow and fast. Tone informs both rhythm and tempo with high and low. And all three of the above are delivery systems for meaning. We want all four things working at the same time. Listen to the acting of others. Is it rhythmically complex? Is it tonally various? Does it contain both fast and slow, or is it flattened out by staying too long in one tempo? And is the actor acting and reacting? Finally, is all of this servicing the line, the scene and the play's meaning? For those of us who love the profession, it is this damnable complexity that keeps us going through thick and thin. Concentrate on one of the four today, but the meaning stays at the center.

SETTING NAMES

Remember that old bugaboo, exposition? Well, in amongst the exposition are people's names, people we're going to meet later, or whose offstage doings are going to impact the narrative. You need to play these names as key words so the next time someone refers to "Billy," the audience knows who he is. Your character may mention "my husband Bill" but thereafter refer only to her "husband." In the next scene, he may enter when you're not there and be simply referred to as "Bill." If you haven't set it the first time, nobody knows he's your husband. Plus, your attitude as you say a character's name for the first time begins to characterize that person for us. Who's who is usually the name of the game in the first 15 pages and, handled sloppily, the audience will be playing catch-up for the whole first act. We want the audience onboard early. Set the names.

GOING VERBAL

There's a lot to the old saw that the audience can't see and hear at the same time. If the text is verbally complex and demanding, we probably shouldn't be waving our arms around simultaneously. When you're acting verse or Shaw or Eric Overmyer or Mac Wellman or other language-based playwrights, restrain your physical work. Enjoy the language and give it center stage. If you're moving restlessly about, chopping out gestures, or writhing in your chair, we aren't going to be able to follow the acrobatics of the language. All of this falls in the category of recognizing what sort of play you are in and using the acting tools that suit it. All acting truths aren't for all markets. Rein in the physical and put the resulting energy into the words. Let them dance while the body sits this one out. I'm not proposing a physical catatonia or a game of talking statues, I am suggesting that we be aware of the balance between the physical and the verbal and the text. What play are you in?

"Then . . . then . . . then he took off his shirt," or, "Billy . . . Billy, where are you? Billy?" Okay, here's something where there's a rule. Don't say them all the same. We need three separate actions or tactics, or to put it bluntly—tonalities. Now this sort of line is a commonplace in most scripts. If the repeated words aren't in one sentence, they may be used three times in three sentences, and there, the context will guide the variety. This, like almost every other practical rule actors have known since Moliere, is in the service of *variety*. The various actor is the better actor. Once again, you need to reach for your indispensable set of colored pencils and note where these repeated words lie. They are easy to overlook in rehearsal, and lack of attention can flatten out a key moment. Words laced throughout a play (as *death* is in *Romeo and Juliet*) have thematic importance, and the whole cast needs to understand that.

MOVEMENT IN SPACE

You're not always going to be acting on giant proscenium stages. Sometimes you'll find yourself doing *Henry IV-Part I* in a theatre which was previously the storage shed behind the Air Devils' Inn. This stage might be 8'x10', and it demands a different physical style. An odd thing happens in these constricted circumstances—the actor becomes tentative as if he felt like the proverbial "bull in a china shop." Remember that you must still handle this space firmly, confidentially and energetically. If it's only three steps from the sofa to the front door, don't shorten the steps. Operate as if you were in a full-sized space. Movement still needs to be purposeful; otherwise you will unwittingly seem halfhearted, and it will sap the acting energy in a dangerous way. The tentative move is a situational or character choice, it must not become a commonplace, and the small acting spaces can be seductive. Don't scale the physical work to the size of the floor.

SPACE

In realistic plays, the actor links space to behavior, as in: I need my coat; it's over the chair. In any other sort of play, the actor links space to metaphor, as in: the truck driver and the debutante declare their love thirty feet apart. Different worlds. The actor also uses space as a sculptor or dancer, carving it with the body to beautiful effect. There is also the use of space for physical punctuation of the text. Books can and are being written on the actor in space. What we need to know right now is to use it purposefully, use it to complete actions, use it to demonstrate psychology. If you don't need it to make a point, don't use it—sit still. Many times, we waste space thinking movement in and of itself is somehow "theatrical." Movement is no more theatrical than stillness. Movement is made theatrical through purpose. Don't use it if you don't have one.

Sniffing

There is always that early part of key scenes when the battle is not yet joined. If it's a love scene, people are testing whether and in what way to declare themselves. If it is a conflict, the antagonists are feeling out each other's strengths and weaknesses, not yet engaging their best troops nor fully disclosing their battle plan. Characters try ploys, attitudes and positions, but delicately, leaving avenues of escape. There is a strange neutrality to their tone even though the line may be loaded with subtext. It is this part of the scene that may easily be overacted, where we have to be careful not to tip our acting hand too early. Try things out on the other character without revealing your final position. Leave yourself plenty of room to grow in the scene. Make sure you're not using up responses and judgments the character will need later in the text. Do less—it's early.

Entering

When you make an entrance, know what has happened to that character in the five minutes before she enters. When you make an entrance, bring new energy on the stage to draw focus and set the terms for the coming scene. When you make an entrance, have some simple task to fulfill immediately (like putting down the groceries). When you make an entrance, make sure whatever stops the move has a point that pertains to someone already on the stage. Own the stage when you enter it. Take a moment to look around and actually see things in and on the set. It will center you. Remember that because you are a complex, sophisticated human who has lived a rich and diverse life, you are worth the money that this audience has paid to see you. Bring an action on with you; don't wait to start one till you're there. Enter.

EXITING

First of all, pay attention to the technique they were probably using on the Roman stage. Get within two steps of wherever you plan to exit before the exit line. The long exit of more than three or four feet is only used to make a very specific point. Also, if the door is going to click or slam, either do it before anyone else speaks or after, so that you don't obscure a key word or phrase. You may want to have your hand on the doorhandle before the exit line, then it goes: open door, say line, exit and close door. For variety, try exiting as you say the final line with the slam as your period. Make sure the action you are playing on the exit carries you all the way out and that we sense you have something to do after the door closes. Remember that those still on the stage will be using your exit as a stimulus, so give them what they need. Leaving is sometimes meant to be memorable . . . was it? Oh, and don't catch your hand in the door. It hurts.

PHYSICAL LINE

We're talking about the body in space. The actor needs to be aware of his or her geometry, in relation to the geometry of the setting and the architecture of the theatre. Look around you. The horizontal of the top of the couch directly behind you could be made dynamic by your body creating a diagonal cutting across it. If the line is a vertical (as in a door jam), you could create an interesting angle by leaning against it. In film, the great directors make compositions frame by frame. On the stage, is this only the director's prerogative? Absolutely not. To begin with, not every director has a strongly developed eye. Sit out in front of the set and take in the composition before you. What does your body add? Often, it's not a matter of changing the blocking but simply adjusting the line of your body. Remember that moving, standing and sitting on the stage is usually behavioral but also consists of elements of line. There is no reason we can't have behavior and a visual aesthetic at the same time. Oh, and use the diagonal—it's the easiest way to improve composition.

BRINGING BLOCKING

All right, you're up from the table and on your feet. The most important thing is to have instincts. When your body wants to move, move! The director's nightmare is actors standing around like "Night of the Living Dead," waiting constantly to be "given" blocking. Now, don't feel badly if the director adjusts what you've brought, but for God's sake don't become passive. Blocking, please remember, is the outward manifestation of inner life, the action and the metaphor. On the one hand—it is behavioral, and on the other hand—it is psychological, as in "I just can't sit here a moment longer." The more you know about the scene, the more the situation interests you; the clearer your action, the more creatively your body will be driven to make blocking (and don't forget our old friend, stillness). Oh, and though I've said it, I'll say it again: write it down! Most directors are working spontaneously, and if you don't remember, they won't either!

SEEING THE PART IN THE BODY

When I'm watching scenework, I sometimes raise my hands to my eyes so that I'm only seeing the actor from the shoulders down. It becomes surprisingly apparent that the impulse that radiates in the actor's face may not reach the rest of the body. The face is alive, but the body is dead. Obviously, the actor's instrument needs to be responding to stimulus in the scene all the way down to the toes. Sports help. Dance training helps. Mime helps. Most of all, the actor needs to keep raising the stakes and sending the shock waves of what they need and what's stopping them from getting it throughout the nervous system. What do my arms, my hands, my waist, my knees, my feet have to say about this moment? You can sometimes drag the rest of your body into the acting process by insisting your feet react. Stamp, kick, shuffle, dance your way through a rehearsal. Concentrate on your feet, and your lower body has no choice but to come with. We don't want to become the stage version of talking heads.

224

BREAK THE STRAIGHT LINE

There is a sort of blocking we've all seen and done that comes to have a murderously mechanical look. The cross goes from the chair to the window, straight as an arrow From there the actor moves as if on a chalk line to the door. On and on it goes, vertically, horizontally and on the angle, one straight cross after another. When asked why, the actor or director replies, "Because, it's the shortest, quickest, most logical route." Quite so, and the most boring and predictable. In the first split second of the move, we know exactly where it's going. Not a good thing dramatically. What to do? Complicate the thought process that accompanies the cross. Go a few steps, decide for a split second you won't go, and then go anyway. Start one way and then decide to go another way. Stop for a second lost in thought. Anything to put a touch of the unexpected in the cross. The next time, take the straight route; you'll have earned it. Personally, I like the arc better than the straight line, it's shapelier and more interesting. Just don't endlessly straight line us to death.

VACILLATION

There is nothing more interesting onstage than to see a man or woman caught between two equally powerful forces. Behind one door—a murderer; behind the other—a sheer drop. She moves one way and then another. We feel in her physicality a psyche poised on a knife's edge. Now this is drama! Another version is, "I want to kiss you, but I shouldn't, but I want to, but I shouldn't." Our lives are filled with these less explosive variations of vacillation and they are the actor's friend. For one thing, vacillation provides physical and mental variety, and we know just how crucial variety is to the actor. The difficulty of choice is the nature of drama. These vacillations also provide the counterpoint for the moment when action becomes decisive. Search your script for these moments where competing pressures (both internal and external) could make you do this . . . or that . . . and then vacillate between the choices, and watch the role vibrate!

SIX THINGS ABOUT SPACE

1. Use it up. Are there parts of the set you're working on you never relate to?
2. Rhythm in space. The patterns and behavior that constitute blocking also have a rhythm. In many cases, it doesn't hurt to think of theatre as dance.
3. Think of space not only horizontally but vertically. Is there a way to do some acting above the stage floor?
4. How does your character's use of space define him? How does a use of space define a relationship?
5. If your character "knows" the space, that character needs to "own" the space. How can you make the space yours?
6. All use of space isn't simply behavior. Some is emotion made manifest, or, as Artaud put it, "signaling through the flames."

THE MIND / BODY CONNECTION

Don't let the idea, the impulse, stop in your head. Get that idea expressed physically. My definition of talent has a lot to do with how much of the actor's body responds to the character's mind. In the good actor, the idea serves as an earthquake that shakes them to their toes. They don't just say the line, they express the line through their nervous system. They remember an insult, and you can see it in their feet. The mind stimulates and the body reacts. The thought triggers the emotion, and the emotion flails the hands. Obviously, just as there are people with a weak mind/body connection, there are characters as well. The actor who has this strong link can turn it up or turn it down to suit the narrative situation. Can this connection be improved? Yes. You have to start by consciously telling the ideas to get down into your body. Somebody is going to have to harp on your accomplishing it. Do. It's a pearl of great price.

VETERANS

In your eagerness to project truth and feel your emotions, do not despise the technical means by which you may convey them.

When in doubt, underact! It will save you many embarrassments.

Stick to the through line. Don't add casual, showy ornaments.

You have heard enough about the hardships of acting as a life. But it can bring happiness. There are moments of sheer joy when everything seems to ring true and one sails free as on a magic carpet . . . the euphoria of the stage.

Don't freeze your performance. Allow it to grow a bit during the run in small ways. Listen to the other actors, alert for tiny changes of emphasis; acknowledge them. But if you go too far, the stage manager may whack you!

Technique is indispensable; when mastered you can finally afford to have fun. If everything else fails, instinct may save you; trust your inborn theatrical instinct.

Acting is goal-oriented, problem-solving behavior. What is your character's dilemma; what is she doing to put it right?

The ultimate goal of the work is to make the observer believe what is happening. Whether your emotion is "real" or not is unimportant if they *believe*.

Do your homework. Learn your lines. Think about the work outside rehearsal. Bring new choices to each rehearsal.

Be passionate. The title of "artist" is one that is earned with rigorous effort and continual self- examination.

Once you and the director have defined the role and plotted the journey and its parameters, forget all that and just let it rip.

Always check your fly.

Try not to "invent" the character . . . you've got everything you need . . . read! The character will gradually emerge and the director will guide you from there.

In the script margin, jot down the first letters of words in a sequence that won't seem to stick in your head. Example: "Kinda chunky little girl" . . . KCLG . . . once done, it seldom has to be referred to again.

Don't use a communal dressing room for vocal warms during half hour . . . we need personal focus and quiet, not in-your-face decibels.

No whistling in the dressing room. No saying the name of (or quoting from) "the Scottish play" anywhere in the theatre. It's a tradition!!!

Drop back one step before you come on. The extra "torque" will give you a nice jolt of energy.

Most actors come to realize that there's a point where the actor knows more about the character than the director. A great director will reach that point with you.

Don't whistle in the dressing room.

Listen.

Repetition is your friend. Repetition is your friend.

Don't waste time trying to *make* it "different"; it's always "different."

Listen.

Don't waste time trying to keep it *exactly* the same; it's always different.

Listen.

Repetition is your friend.

Don't whistle in the dressing room.

In the first week of rehearsal, try to read the play every day. This will give you a clear idea of the play's structure, through line of the action and your character's contribution to that action.

If in rehearsal you have questions about your character's motivations or relationships, go back to the script. What you don't find, you have to invent.

If you find yourself confused or uncomfortable in a scene, the best way out of that situation is to watch and listen to the people around you. What is done or said, exactly, to motivate you?

If you have a large emotional scene . . . joy, sorrow, anger, etc . . . . and you and your director have decided it should be underplayed, one time push the scene to its limit. Go all the way. After you have done that, you will know exactly what you are underplaying.

VETERANS

FRED MAJOR

A play is an orchestral piece. At the first read-through, listen for the missing instrument and supply it.

When rehearsing book-in-hand, don't look at the words while you're speaking. Look back whenever you need to, grab a chunk of material, look up and say it.

If everytime you say or do a particular thing there is laughter in rehearsal, be suspicious! It's probably only because they know you.

It's obvious, but always take the costume into account mentally while you rehearse.

The play is about you only as long as the text will bear it. Learn how to help focus and support someone else's moment.

Wear comfortable shoes.

If you go up, relax. You know the line, you just can't find it.

If you miss an entrance, get there as quickly as you can, but don't run backstage in the dark screaming "Shit".

Remember that what we call naturalism is just another style.

Learn your lines; show up on time; and bring your sense of humor.

Yes, I'm afraid it's true. Your body and your voice are your tools. Train them well and keep them that way.

Steal, steal, steal from the best. Watch the great actors and "store."

Work with the best directors and best actors you can find. They will make you look good. But, above all, work. Acting isn't waiting for the big phone call.

Leave your ego in the dressing room. We all want the audience to love us. Try, oh try, to forget that. Do the work of the play. Be courageous. It's worth the struggle.

Less is truly more. Simplicity—stillness (not to be confused with pauses) speaks volumes.

Victor Talmadge

As a young professional actor I roamed backstage looking for any tidbit and inspiration I could find. I noticed one of the more experirence actors waiting just offstage five to ten minutes before his entrance. Too intimidated to ask why, I tried it myself and the results were remarkable. The exercise immediately focused my attention. I carried less tension. I understood the rhythm and interaction between actor and audience. To this day I make it ap oint to give myself as much time as possible in the sings listening and watching the action onstage before I make my entrance.

The actor's spirit, above all, needs something to work on—something tonight, something tomorrow, something the day after that. Our intuition and our instincts are always functioning, but our conscious mind needs grist, a plan, a target for our arrows. What is it you intend to be working on in tomorrow's rehearsal? Now, however you answered that question, you need to relate it to specific pieces of text. Everything we imagine brings us back to the text, and it is to the text we bring our insights, and it is there we find our challenges. When you have an idea, point to the specific part of the text that will allow you to get the idea on stage. You want to make the character "more dependent?" Where is the text that allows that to play? You want to show that she gets progressively "more alienated"; which lines show that progression or allow the subtext that will? You wish to find the seeds of distrust that lead him to leave her? Point to the lines. Too much of our work as actors is free-floating, general, without being found specifically in the words and/or the circumstances. Eventually, all our ideas are given flesh on or around the lines. All the tips you've been reading are meant to lead you back to the script. Have the idea, then find the words to play it with. This, I think, might be the tip of tips.